Investigative Work in the Science Curriculum

DEVELOPING SCIENCE AND TECHNOLOGY EDUCATION

Series Editor: Brian Woolnough,
Department of Educational Studies, University of Oxford

Current titles:

John Eggleston: *Teaching Design and Technology*
Richard Gott and Sandra Duggan: *Investigative Work in the Science Curriculum*
David Layton: *Technology's Challenge to Science Education*
Keith Postlethwaite: *Differentiated Science Teaching*
Michael J. Reiss: *Science Education for a Pluralist Society*
Jon Scaife and Jerry Wellington: *Information Technology in Science and Technology Education*
Joan Solomon: *Teaching Science, Technology and Society*
Clive Sutton: *Words, Science and Learning*
Brian Woolnough: *Effective Science Teaching*

Investigative Work in the Science Curriculum

RICHARD GOTT and SANDRA DUGGAN

Open University Press
Buckingham · Philadelphia

Open University Press
Celtic Court
22 Ballmoor
Buckingham
MK18 1XW

and
1900 Frost Road, Suite 101
Bristol, PA 19007, USA

First published 1995

A catalogue record of this book is available from the British Library

Library of Congress Cataloging-in-Publication Data

Gott, Richard, 1946–
    Investigative work in the science curriculum/Richard Gott,
Sandra Duggan.
        p.   cm. — (Developing science and technology education)
    Includes bibilographical references and index.
    ISBN 0–335–19144–4   ISBN 0–335–19143–6 (pbk.)
    1. Science–Study and teaching–England–Curricula. 2. Curriculum
planning–England. I. Duggan, Sandra, 1949–   . II. Title.
III. Series.
Q183.4.G72E534   1994
507' . 1'241–dc20

This book is based on research commissioned by the National Curriculum
Council and carried out by the Exploration in Science Team at the University
of Durham. The research was directed by Richard Gott. Ken Foulds of
Seaham Comprehensive School, County Durham was the project leader,
responsible for the design and implementation of the project, much of its analysis
and the ensuing research report.

Typeset and illustrated by PanTek Arts, Maidstone, Kent
Printed in Great Britain by St Edmundsbury Press, Bury St Edmunds, Suffolk

Contents

Series editor's preface

It may seem surprising that after three decades of curriculum innovation, and with the increasing provision of a centralised National Curriculum, it is felt necessary to produce a series of books which encourages teachers and curriculum developers to continue to rethink how science and technology should be taught in schools. But teaching can never be merely the 'delivery' of someone else's 'given' curriculum. It is essentially a personal and professional business in which lively, thinking, enthusiastic teachers continue to analyse their own activities and mediate the curriculum framework to their students. If teachers ever cease to be critical of what they are doing, then their teaching, and their students' learning, will become sterile.

There are still important questions which need to be addressed, questions which remain fundamental but the answers to which may vary according to the social conditions and educational priorities at a particular time.

What is the justification for teaching science and technology in our schools? For educational or vocational reasons? Providing science and technology for all, for future educated citizens, or to provide adequately prepared and motivated students to fulfil the industrial needs of the country? Will the same type of curriculum satisfactorily meet both needs or do we need a differentiated curriculum? In the past it has too readily been assumed that one type of science will meet all needs.

What should be the nature of science and technology in schools? It will need to develop both the methods and the content of the subject, the way a scientist or engineer works and the appropriate knowledge and understanding, but what is the relationship between the two? How does the student's explicit knowledge relate to investigational skill, how important is the student's tacit knowledge? In the past the holistic nature of scientific activity and the importance of affective factors such as commitment and enjoyment have been seriously undervalued in relation to the student's success.

And, of particular concern to this series, what is the relationship between science and technology? In some countries the scientific nature of technology and the technological aspects of science make the subjects a natural continuum. In others the curriculum structures have separated the two, leaving the teachers to develop appropriate links. Underlying this series is the belief that science and technology have an important interdependence and thus many of the books will be appropriate to teachers of both science and technology.

There have been few changes in school science teaching over the past few years that have been more significant than the change in the type of practical work being done. Moving from the ubiquitous 'cookery book' type practical, in which the students followed the teacher's recipe, through the 'guided discovery' experiment and the experiments designed to develop and test specific practical skills, we have now the practical investigation where the students are expected to design, deliver and evaluate their own experiment. This move, which had been advocated and practised by a minority since science teaching began, has now been enshrined in the National Curriculum for Science in England and Wales. Though, in this form, it stresses a pure science model of investigation as distinct from a more technological problem-solving type of investigation, it has done much to introduce genuine scientific activity into schools.

Among the most influential in bringing about this change have been Richard Gott and his colleagues, first through his APU work, then in his *Active Science* textbooks, and subsequently by his own research work into the way students and teachers actually do investigations. And it is on this work that this scholarly and perceptive book by Richard Gott and Sandra Duggan has been based. Much of the early discussion about the 'best type' of practical work for schools was based more on rhetoric than on research. This important book is timely, for it spells out in careful and authoritative

detail just what doing investigative work means, how students tackle and develop such work, and how it can be encouraged and assessed. It should go a long way to underpinning investigative practical work so that, despite the logistical difficulties involved in such work, it becomes securely based as the most important type of practical work in schools. Such holistic investigational practical work, whether it is of a pure scientific nature or more technologically problem-solving, is of vital importance. It develops not only the students' knowledge, understanding and practical skills but also the all-important affective aspects of enjoyment, motivation, commitment and self-confidence. I hope and believe that this book will help to deliver such in both science and technology lessons.

Brian E. Woolnough

Foreword

What is this book about?

Some years ago now, one of us (R.G.) was responsible, with others, for the assessment of science investigations for the Assessment of Performance Unit (APU) team based at Leeds University. On moving to Durham, the ideas developed at Leeds were taken into a local school and, over a number of years, incorporated into a workable curriculum. Concurrent with these developments came the National Curriculum. The team at Durham was contracted by the National Curriculum Council (NCC) to undertake research into pupils' ability to carry out investigations in both primary and secondary schools. The aim of the research was, primarily, to inform any subsequent revisions to the structure of the 'investigations' element of science. The experience of using investigations in the classroom, together with the extensive research material gathered for NCC, form the basis of this book.

The structure of the book

This book has evolved in the writing. It arose out of a desire to publish the results of the research. Reflecting on the findings of this research has led us to develop our thinking and moved us forward in two ways: in developing the theoretical model which has been latent in our thinking, and in considering how the implications of the research can be applied in the classroom.

The first chapter locates the changing role of practical work historically. The reader is advised that it would be unwise to omit the second chapter, which focuses on the theoretical framework, since it discusses the thinking which underlies much of the rest of the book. The research findings are confined to Chapters 4 and 5, while Chapters 6, 7, 8 and 9 are concerned with teaching and assessment.

Acknowledgements

We would like to acknowledge the assistance and support of a number of people during the process of writing this book: Ken Foulds and Rosemary Feasey for their discussions of the NCC project work; Helen Costello for the useful discussions and her support and advice throughout the development of the book; all those people who have taken the time and trouble to read and comment on the manuscript, including Ruth Jarman (Queen's University, Belfast) and members of the Exploration of Science team in Durham. We would also like to thank Philip Adey for his comments on Chapter 2; our respective partners for their comments on the manuscript and their forbearance; and, last but not least, the rest of our families – for their patience.

The authors and publishers would also like to acknowledge the following for permission to reproduce material: Taylor and Francis, Newton D.P. and Newton L.D. (drawing on p. 141) and the Northamptonshire Inspection and Advisory Service (Table 7.4.). Figures 1.2, 1.3 and Table 8.3 are reproduced by permission of Simon and Schuster Education, Hemel Hempstead, UK.

Glossary

Application	putting knowledge to use in an unfamiliar or novel situation.
Categoric variable	a variable which is defined descriptively, e.g. shape, colour, type of material.
Concepts	substantive concepts – the facts, laws, theories and principles of science (e.g. gravity, photosynthesis, solubility). Also known as declarative concepts. concepts of evidence – the concepts associated with procedural understanding. They include for instance the concept of the fair test, identification of variables as independent and dependent, validity and reliability.
Conceptual understanding	the understanding of substantive concepts (see above).
Continuous variable	a variable which is defined numerically and which can take any value, e.g. height.
Control variable	the variable(s) which must be kept constant while the independent variable is changed in order to keep the test 'fair'.
Dependent variable	the variable which changes, and is measured or judged, each time the independent variable is changed.
Derived variable	a variable which is derived from more than one measurement, e.g. speed or rate.
Discrete variable	a variable which is defined numerically but which takes only integer values, e.g. number of layers of insulation material (cf. continuous variable).
Epistemology	the methodology or basis for knowledge.
Exploration	a very open kind of task, where pupils are given the context only and allowed to raise their own questions and then follow these up to find the answer. This could involve practical work, surveys or a library search. It will include problem-solving (and investigations).

Heuristic method	a system of education in which the pupil is 'taught' to find out things for him/herself.
Independent variable	the value chosen and manipulated by the investigator.
Investigation	a specific type of problem-solving defined as 'a task for which a pupil cannot immediately see an answer or recall a routine method for finding it.'
Key Stages	the four age ranges encompassed by the UK National Curriculum: Key Stage 1, 5–7-year-olds; Key Stage 2, 7–11-year-olds; Key Stage 3, 11–14-year-olds; and Key Stage 4, 14–16-year-olds.
Problem-solving	the solving of problems, i.e. any activity that requires pupils to apply their understanding in a new situation. Investigations are one type of problem-solving.
Procedural understanding	the understanding required in knowing how to do science. It is defined here as the understanding and application of (skills and) concepts of evidence. Procedural understanding is complementary to conceptual understanding.
Processes	the cognitive processes associated with any intellectual activity including the solving of scientific problems. They include hypothesising, interpreting, predicting, etc.
Programme of study	in the UK National Curriculum, the required teaching for each key stage.
Skills	those activities which are necessary but not sufficient in themselves to the carrying out of most practical work, e.g. the mechanics of the use of measuring instruments, how to construct a graph.
Substantive structure	the structure of science concerned with its declarative concepts (see also substantive concepts).
Syntactic structure	the structure of skills and concepts of evidence (see above) describing how skills and concepts of evidence are put together to solve a problem (cf. syntax in language).
Synthesis	the putting together of separate bits of knowledge into a connected whole so that a new structure emerges.
Understanding	the ability to explain and interpret information within a given context (cf. application).
Variables	any observation which can be described by different values, e.g. the colour of a bird, length or weight.

Abbreviations

APU	Assessment of Performance Unit
APWIS	Assessment of Practical Work in Science
AT	Attainment Targets in the UK National Curriculum – 'things which pupils should know, understand or be able to do'
NCC	National Curriculum Council
OPENS	the Open-ended work in Science project funded by the Department of Education and Science
Sc1	the attainment target in the UK National Curriculum which focuses on investigations
SEAC	Schools Examination and Assessment Council

CHAPTER 1

Changing views of practical science

The emergence of practical science

Early beginnings

To discover why investigations have come to occupy the position that they now hold within practical science, we must first go back in time and consider the emergence of practical work within the science curriculum. In other words, before we can answer the question 'Why do investigations?', we must ask 'Why do practical work at all?'

The historical origins of practical work in science have been well documented by Gee and Clackson (1992). Briefly, practical work began to emerge in England soon after the Great Exhibition of 1851 when state support grants were made available and the Department of Science and Art was established in 1854. Money was provided to set up and equip school science laboratories, although the emphasis in these early days was very much on demonstrations by the teacher with a clear focus on the illustration of particular concepts. The increasing recognition that practical work was essential in science education stemmed primarily from two schools of thought: the recognition of the social and economic importance of science, and the philosophical arguments which had arisen from the works of Huxley and Spencer and were now being developed by Armstrong. Armstrong advocated the 'heuristic' approach, in which the pupil is trained to find out things for him/herself. It is based on a belief in the effectiveness of learning through action as opposed to the passive assimila-

tion of knowledge. Armstrong (1896:42) believed that: 'Knowledge alone is not power; but the knowledge how to use knowledge is.'

Armstrong held what would now be considered to be somewhat extreme views in which he considered lectures and textbooks in a rather negative light to say the least, urging his students:

> Don't look at a text-book: avoid most of them as
> you would poison. Their methods are as a rule
> detestable and destructive of all honest effort
> towards development of powers of selfhelpful-
> ness...you must never be satisfied with lectures
> alone if you wish to do more than spend your time
> pleasantly...the student of any branch of natural
> science must go to the bench and work hard there.
> (Armstrong, 1896:43,50)

This precipitated a move towards encouraging individual practical work in schools, in the way that we now take for granted.

However, by the turn of the century, the heuristic movement was beginning to fall out of favour because it had assumed that scientific concepts could be discovered by 'common sense'. As scientific knowledge increased, this idea was no longer tenable. At the same time, there was evidence from experimental psychologists suggesting that the transfer of training in scientific method from one problem to another was not, as Armstrong had assumed, a common occurrence (see, for instance, Wellington, 1989). As a result, the pendulum swung towards 'content' and away from the emphasis on 'method'. Wellington describes how the humanising influence of science was promoted at this time, since it was felt that it had previously been ignored and that 'science was to be taught for the benefit of the learner and not for the benefit of science itself'.

We shall return to these ideas later when we consider the notion of 'audience' in the next chapter and its influence on what children perceive as the purpose of collecting data from experimental work. However, the consequence of this pupil-centred approach to science education was that the status of practical work *per se* was lower than it had previously been and subservient to theory and content. Most of the practical work at that time consisted of following 'recipes' to verify theory or to illustrate concepts and, towards the end of this period, there was growing concern that much of this practical work was routine and repetitive. Nevertheless, practical work had already established itself as a vital part of the science curriculum in that there was no longer any great argument as to its desirability, albeit in a supporting role, in the classroom or laboratory.

The Nuffield schemes

While practical work in science was and continues to be regarded as essential, its precise purpose is much less certain. In 1959, the Kerr inquiry was commissioned to inquire into the nature *and purpose* of practical work in school science teaching in England and Wales. The report found that:

> When science students were asked about the influence of practical work done at school, few of them thought the finding-out element had been given an important place nor were they particularly aware of being led towards a scientific way of thinking and behaving. The members of the Inquiry Team think a much more direct and deliberate attempt should be made to teach for these ends through practical work. No aspect of science education is more urgently in need of attention.
>
> (Kerr, 1964:95)

Thus the pendulum swung back again towards a practical science which not only included illustrative practicals, but which placed an emphasis on those where pupils could 'find out' by discovery and those which enabled students to practise 'scientific method'. Hence the influential Nuffield schemes for secondary pupils (years 7–13) were born. It almost seemed as if Armstrong's heurism was back. Again the intention was that pupils should be encouraged to *discover science for themselves*. The focus was on scientific method and objectivity with an underlying assumption that the pupil had no preconceptions (the inductivist stance), so that all observations were perceived as neutral. The essence of the Nuffield philosophy was 'to awaken the spirit of investigation *and to develop disciplined imaginative thinking*' (Nuffield Foundation, 1966).

This explicit recognition of the importance of cognitive processes is perhaps one of the most significant elements of the underlying philosophy of the Nuffield schemes. However, while the renewed emphasis on 'finding out' and scientific methodology was welcomed by educationists generally, once the Nuffield schemes were implemented, certain fundamental problems emerged. The most significant problem was that because the activities were relatively tightly controlled and the 'right answer' often apparent, there was little scope for 'discovery' in the true sense of the word. Hence, Nuffield practicals were often contrived and the spirit of 'imaginative thinking' was lost. The detail of the practical was not considered to be important because it was so carefully controlled and indeed much of the equipment was designed so that little could go wrong – in theory at least. It was only at the higher levels, such as in investigational projects of the Nuffield A level physics course, that there was an element which allowed pupils a less structured format. Here, there were investigations where the outcome in terms of pupils' performance was less certain. However, for the majority, the reality was that Nuffield practicals were about illustrating or refining concepts rather than 'finding out', despite a clearly stated philosophy in the teachers' guides which advocated a very open approach.

The schemes were well supported financially, but this in itself had disadvantages because it meant that some schools jumped on the Nuffield bandwagon without really understanding its ethos. More importantly, because the O and A level science schemes received priority, the Nuffield schemes were originally designed for the most able grammar school pupils. With the advent of the comprehensive system, problems arose. When the Nuffield schemes were used in comprehensive schools, the conceptual nature of the whole course was simply too much for the majority. Many of us, the authors included, who had worked with the Nuffield schemes in a grammar school environment, slowly – too slowly probably – passed from unease to the realisation that such a course was not, and could not be, for the many. And since, in the comprehensive, the few for whom the course was designed were now very few indeed, alternatives had to be found. There were eventually attempts to address this problem (for example, with the publication of the Nuffield Secondary Science Teaching Project in 1971), but they were not entirely successful. Alexander (1974), in evaluating this project, found that: 'the lessons showed a high degree of structure and relatively little work of a completely open ended nature...pupils' attitudes to science and to the relevance of science in society had not improved'. This last point, that Nuffield science had no obvious link to the world outside the school laboratory, was also a general criticism of all the Nuffield schemes.

In summary, the Nuffield schemes began with a clear intention of teaching scientific method, but in practice their main purpose was still to teach the concepts of scientific knowledge. The practicals were based on the notion that 'seeing is believing'. It gradually became clear that these 'guided-discovery' practicals were not achieving the original aims of the Nuffield schemes. Qualter *et al.* (1990) write:

> We have only to look at schemes such as Nuffield Combined Science to realise that a great deal of time, energy and material resources are devoted to 'guiding' the pupil to a predetermined 'discovery'. Critics of such schemes have questioned whether such a massive investment of resources is really justified by such narrowly defined learning objectives.

The 'processes and skills' movement

In 1967, a scheme arose in America called 'Science – A Process Approach' (SAPA; see American Association for the Advancement of Science, 1967). It stemmed from a study of what scientists actually do in their everyday work. SAPA placed a firm emphasis on scientific method or 'process', regarding the 'substantive' concepts of science – that is, the facts, laws and principles – as being far less important. Other schemes of the same ilk soon emerged and thus the 'processes and skills' movement was born.

It should be noted here that there has been, and continues to be, much confusion over the terms 'processes', 'process skills', 'procedures' and 'methods'. In science education, these terms are often used interchangeably without clear definition, causing considerable problems. In the processes and skills movement, 'processes' were intended to refer not to the practical *skills* associated with science, but to the *cognitive* processes such as observing, classifying and inferring – that is, the thoughts that go through scientists' minds as they perform practical science activities. This is the meaning we shall adopt here. It follows that the term 'process skills' which was widely used at that time, is a contradiction in terms, confusing the cognitive process element with the practical skill element. Some of the problems encountered by the process movement can be seen to stem from this lack of clarity of definition as well as an uncertainty about the place of these processes in school science generally.

In the UK, Screen (1986) suggested that the swing from content to process was aided by the advent of new national criteria for science syllabi and assessment in 1986. Prior to that time, both the Nuffield schemes and the concern about meeting examination requirements had led teachers to concentrate on facts and knowledge. A policy document in 1985 stated that: 'The essential characteristic of education in science is that it introduces pupils to the *methods* of science so that scientific competence can be developed to the full' (DES, 1985). Screen, the author of a processes and skills scheme called Warwick

Process Science, further argued that: 'It could be said that the most valuable elements of a scientific education are those that remain after the facts have been forgotten' (Screen, 1986). And again: 'important though the content of science might be, it is not the facts themselves but how they are arrived at which constitutes an education in science' (Screen, 1988). There was now a feeling that factual scientific knowledge was so abundant (indeed Screen uses the term 'the explosion of knowledge'), that very few students could possibly acquire a thorough knowledge of any subject area. Instead, students needed to know how 'to access, use and ultimately add to the information store when required' (Screen 1986).

The focus of Warwick Process Science was therefore on transferable 'process skills', which included observing, classifying and interpreting. Screen points to two other advantages of this process-led scheme. First, 'process skills' are not only useful in practising science but also in questioning the practice of other scientific work. Second, the scheme allows the teacher to observe pupils' conceptions and misconceptions in lessons where, for example, the focus is on predicting, hypothesising or interpreting. The teacher can then use this information to address misconceptions.

Similarly, a new Nuffield scheme emerged around this time in which 'emphasis has been placed on processes...on process rather than products' (Nuffield Foundation, 1987). There are also a number of assessment schemes, such as The Assessment of Practical Science (TAPS; Bryce *et al.*, 1983) and the Graded Assessment in Science Project (GASP; Davis, 1989), based on the assessment of 'process'.

In general, schemes that adopt this process approach aim to consider, as far as is possible, one process at a time as the focus of a lesson. The practical work then serves to illustrate the process in question. Bryce *et al.* (1983) base their scheme on the idea that: 'pupils are encouraged to master basic skills first and are thereby enabled to progress to more complex process skills and eventually practical investigations'. Woolnough (1991) contrasts this 'step-by-step' approach with the question: '...do they [the pupils] learn best by a

holistic, experiential approach whereby they are encouraged to do small, complete investigations from the earliest stage, progressing to more difficult investigations later and picking up appropriate skills when necessary?'

With the process approach, problems can arise in trying to incorporate these processes into a coherent scheme of work. Process schemes have also been criticised for their content because the concepts they employ to focus on different processes often lack continuity. There is indeed the real possibility that learning processes in isolation may mean that some pupils will have difficulty in putting them all together appropriately when required to do so. Process-led science cannot, of course, be devoid of content, but its emphasis is clearly on the processes practised in the context of science: 'Science in Process...is based on the processes of science – on how to work scientifically – rather than on a body of content' (Wray *et al.*, 1987).

Investigations

After the processes and skills movement came a move towards the holistic approach referred to by Woolnough (1991) in the form of scientific 'investigation'. This move was driven by the work of the Assessment of Performance Unit's (APU) work in science and subsequently by the inclusion of investigative work in the UK National Curriculum. In the next section, we shall provide an example of an investigation and in Chapter 3 we shall define investigations in depth by considering different types of investigations. Suffice it to say here that investigations are a specific type of problem-solving which allow pupils a varying degree of autonomy and which are problems to which the solution is not obvious. Investigations aim to allow pupils to use and apply *both concepts and cognitive processes*, as well as practical skills. This book sets out to show that this is a more balanced view of science, which can be seen perhaps as a response to the extremes of the past. Various schemes have arisen in recent years in the UK which have focused on investigations (Foulds *et al.*, 1990,

Table 1.1 Summary of types of practical work

Type of practical	Aim
Skills	To acquire a particular skill
Observation	To provide opportunities for pupils to use their conceptual framework in relating real objects and events to scientific ideas
Enquiry	To discover or acquire a concept, law or principle
Illustration	To 'prove' or verify a particular concept, law or principle
Investigation	To provide opportunities for pupils to use concepts, cognitive processes and skills to solve a problem

1993; Feasey *et al.*, 1991) and their integration into the practical science curriculum.

Practical science today

What kinds of practical work in science are used in today's schools? If we adopt a bird's-eye view of all the school laboratories in action in the UK today, we would find a large variety of types of practical science being carried out which stem from the history we have just described. There has been, and still is, a tendency to regard practical work as one amorphous entity. By uncovering what different types of practicals set out to teach, we shall see that this is not the case and that each type of practical serves a different purpose.

Various attempts have been made to classify different kinds of practical work in order to define their respective roles. We shall consider here a classification developed by Gott *et al.* (1988), which consists of five broad types of practical work (Table 1.1). The boundaries between these types are not claimed to be watertight; practical activities can clearly include more than one aspect, particularly skills and observation which are implicit to some degree in the other types.

Enquiry practicals are structured to allow the pupils to discover a particular concept for themselves. Such experiments have to be carefully set up to enable all pupils to arrive at the same endpoint. Many of the Nuffield practicals followed this format. The main aim of enquiry practicals is concept acquisition.

Illustrative practicals differ in that they aim to demonstrate or provide a particular concept, law or principle, which has already been introduced by the teacher, to allow the pupil to 'see' the concept in action and so relate theory more closely to reality. Illustrative practicals can take the form of a demonstration by the teacher or a practical where pupils are given detailed instructions or a 'recipe' to follow. The main aim of illustration is concept consolidation. The spring's activity in Fig. 1.1 is a typical practical where the pupils either 'discover' Hooke's Law in an enquiry practical, or if it follows directed teaching on the topic, the same activity can be used as an illustrative practical enabling pupils to see the concept in action.

Skills practicals may involve setting up, reading and using instruments as in the example taken from Gott *et al.* (1988) and reproduced as Fig. 1.2, or they might require pupils to learn and practise the construction of line graphs or bar charts. They are about acquiring the basic skills necessary for carrying out the rest of practical science. Once acquired, the skill of constructing a graph from a data set comes as second nature. The collection of the data and the interpretation of the graph are of a different order and are not within *our* definition of skills.

Observation in science has been described as 'theory-laden' in that when pupils are asked to

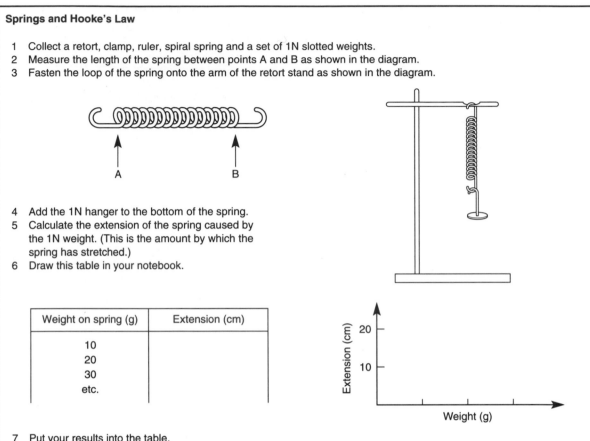

Springs and Hooke's Law

1 Collect a retort, clamp, ruler, spiral spring and a set of 1N slotted weights.
2 Measure the length of the spring between points A and B as shown in the diagram.
3 Fasten the loop of the spring onto the arm of the retort stand as shown in the diagram.

4 Add the 1N hanger to the bottom of the spring.
5 Calculate the extension of the spring caused by the 1N weight. (This is the amount by which the spring has stretched.)
6 Draw this table in your notebook.

Weight on spring (g)	Extension (cm)
10	
20	
30	
etc.	

7 Put your results into the table.
8 Find the extension of the spring for weights of 2N, 3N, 4N and 5N. Add your results to the table each time.
9 Use your results to draw a graph using these axes.
10 What conclusions can you draw from this experiment?

Fig. 1.1 An example of an enquiry or illustration practical

observe in science they are expected to apply scientific conceptual knowledge to the object or event in question. Hence in the example shown in Fig. 1.3, again from Gott *et al.* (1988), the teacher is asking pupils to apply ideas such as conduction and condensation to the observed phenomena.

Investigations usually offer several alternative ways of reaching a solution to the problem so that the design is much less controlled than in illustrative or enquiry work. Investigations use concepts which have been introduced by some other means; in an illustrative practical or exposition perhaps. Their main aim is to allow pupils to use concepts,

cognitive processes and skills to solve a problem. An example from *Investigations in Science* (Foulds *et al.*, 1990) of an investigation called 'On the tiles' sets the scene as follows:

It was chaos in the kitchen! The baby had dropped his bottle and milk was dripping out. Little Rachel knocked her plate off the table – the bread landed jam-side down. In from the garden came Dad – with muddy boots on. He was followed by Sparky the dog, who had just been digging for bones. The floor was really messy. How easy will it be to clean up?

Slide making

1 Use the pipette to place a medium-sized drop of the pond water from beaker A onto the centre of a clean slide.

2 Cover with a coverslip taking care to exclude air bubbles.

3 Use a strip of blotting paper to remove excess water from the slide.

4 Place the finished slide onto the microscope stage so that the water drop is in the centre of the field of view.

5 Focus the microscope at low power.

6 Put up your hand for your teacher to check your slide.

7 Write down what you see in the pond water when you use the microscope.

Fig. 1.2 An example of a skills practical

Icecan

In front of you is a tin can with a mixture of ice and water in it.

(a) Look carefully at the outside of the can. What do you notice?

_____

_____

_____

(b) Say why you think those things happened

_____

_____

_____

Fig. 1.3 An example of an observation practical

The pupils are then asked: 'to find out which is the best material for covering the kitchen floor', but before they begin each group is asked to write one sentence explaining what 'best' means. Foulds *et al.* (1990) suggest that the different interpretations of 'best' could then be discussed by the class to decide what course the investigation follows. Some guidance is given on structuring the recording:

Your results might be easier to read in a table. Before you draw the columns and headings, think about what goes in them – think about how many types of covering you will use, what you will put on it, what name you will give to your measurements, etc.

(Foulds *et al.*, 1990)

Summary

In this chapter, we have traced the historical development of practical science and seen that it has offered several different views of its role and purpose. We have seen that, over the last 150 years, there have been quite radical swings. The earliest practical work focused on concepts, while Armstrong's heurism swung the pendulum firmly towards the processes of science. The Nuffield schemes were intended to follow this trend but in practice focused on concept acquisition, while the processes and skills movement swung the pendulum back again. The move towards investigations seems to lie somewhere in the middle.

If we have anything to learn from history in this context, it must surely be that we should avoid these radical swings that have occurred in the past. In the not too distant past, it often seemed as if there were fashions in practical science – when one scheme came in, the previous one was thrown out. There has also been a competitive element between schools, suggesting that one scheme was 'better' at teaching the practical component of science than another.

A further related problem is that there has been a tendency for teachers to accept that doing practical work regularly is a 'good thing', with little thought as to its purpose or learning outcomes. It is as if all practical work is one amorphous entity serving a kind of 'hands-on' purpose in the curriculum. Hodson (1992) suggests that a lot of what goes under the name of practical science is 'muddled and without real educational value'. He cites evidence (Hodson, 1990) to show that the reasons different teachers give for doing practical work are diverse. Hodson argues that the teacher must be precise about the required learning outcome of the lesson and then decide whether practical work is the best way of achieving that goal. This leads him to question the whole purpose of practical work. We have used one classification here to unravel the purposes of different kinds of practical work. Hodson suggests that computer-assisted learning (CAL) can be used to learn concepts and theories and to learn about the nature of science, but when it comes to 'doing science', he writes:

> A major goal of practical work should be the engagement of students in holistic investigations in which they use the processes of science both to explore and develop their conceptual understanding and to acquire a deeper understanding of (and increased expertise in) scientific practice.
>
> (Hodson, 1992)

To conclude, we have painted a picture of the current state of practical work, which suggests that there is a lack of clear thinking behind its present rather disjointed and inconsistent structure. Perhaps we need to stand back and try to develop a framework to enable us to locate and pull all these ideas about the purpose and nature of practical work together. That framework should begin the task of deciding what different sorts of practical work are for and when, how and why they should be deployed, rather than either letting them co-exist in a muddle or, worse, assuming that the latest type is a competitor which is to supplant or be defeated by other types. We shall then be able to locate investigations within that framework so that their role in the science curriculum becomes clear and so that we can then move on to explore investigative work itself.

References

Alexander, D.J. (1974). *Nuffield Secondary Science: An Evaluation*. London, Macmillan.

American Association for the Advancement of Science (1967). *Science – A Process Approach*. Washington, DC, Ginn & Co.

Armstrong, H.E. (1896). How science must be studied to be useful. From 'The Technical World', in *H.E. Armstrong and Science Education* (1973; G. Van Praagh, ed.). London, John Murray.

Bryce, T.G.K., McCall, J., MacGregor, J., Robertson, I.J. and Weston, R.A.J. (1983). *Techniques for the Assessment of Practical Skills in Foundation Science*. London, Heinemann.

Davis, B.C. (1989). *GASP: Graded Assessment in Science Project*. London, Hutchinson.

Department of Education and Science (1985). *Science 5–16: A Statement of Policy*. London, HMSO.

Feasey, R., Foulds, K., Gott, R. and Pryke, T. (1991). *Science in Action 5 to 16: Key Stage 3*, Book 1. Glasgow, Nelson Blackie.

Foulds, K., Mashiter, J. and Gott, R. (1990). *Investigations in Science*. Glasgow, Blackie.

Foulds, K., Gott, R., Pryke, T. and Borrows, P. (1993). *Science in Action 5 to 16: Key Stage 3*, Book 2. Glasgow, Nelson Blackie.

Gee, B. and Clackson, S.G. (1992). The origin of practical work in the English school science curriculum. *School Science Review*, 73(265): 79–83.

Gott, R., Welford, G. and Foulds, K. (1988). *The Assessment of Practical Work in Science*. Oxford, Blackwell.

Hodson, D. (1990). A critical look at practical work in school science. *School Science Review*, 70(256): 33–40.

Hodson, D. (1992). Redefining and reorienting practical work in school science. *School Science Review*, 73(264) 65–78.

Kerr, J.F. (1964). *Practical Work in School Science*. Leicester, Leicester University Press.

Nuffield Foundation (1966). *Nuffield Chemistry: Introduction and Guide*. Harlow, Longman/Penguin.

Nuffield Foundation (1987). *Nuffield 11 to 13 Science: Teacher's Guide 2. How Science is Used*. Harlow, Longman.

Qualter, A., Strang, J., Swatton, P. and Taylor, R. (1990). *Exploration: A Way of Learning Science*. Oxford, Blackwell.

Screen, P.A. (1986). The Warwick Process science project. *School Science Review*, 72(260): 17–24.

Screen, P.A. (1988). A case for a process approach: The Warwick experience. *Physics Education*, 23: 146–9.

Wellington, J. (ed.) (1989). *Skills and Processes in Science Education*. London, Routledge.

Woolnough, B.E. (1991). Setting the scene. In: *Practical Science* (B.E. Woolnough, ed.). Buckingham, Open University Press.

Wray, J., Freeman, J., Campbell, L., Hoyle, P., Nimenko, G., Smyth, S. and Whiston, L. (1987). *Science in Process. Teachers' Resource Pack*. London, Heinemann Educational Books.

CHAPTER 2

Alternative perspectives

In this chapter, we shall attempt to gather the ideas behind the various types of practical work described in Chapter 1 into a coherent framework which allows them to be seen as complementary rather than competing views of science. Such a framework, incorporating ideas about the nature and purpose of practical work, must relate to school science as a whole. Practical work should be an integral part of the science curriculum which mirrors, reinforces and augments the rest of the course.

In the first part of this chapter, we present and then develop a model and a taxonomy (or classification) which are applicable to the whole of the science curriculum as well as to practical science. They are based on an epistemological perspective, which seeks to define that which is to be taught and learned, rather than how that is to occur. This perspective underlies much of the following chapters. In the second part of the chapter, we consider the movement towards teaching thinking skills, which regards education from a psychological perspective. We will look in particular at the Cognitive Acceleration through Science Education (CASE) project, which teaches thinking skills through the science curriculum.

A 'content' perspective (an epistemological view)

A model of science

A model based on that advanced by Gott and Mashiter (1991) will serve as a starting point in our search for a coherent framework (Fig. 2.1). It should be noted that this model was a basic, and deliberately simplified, model for science and not solely for practical science. Here the cognitive processes (which we defined in the last chapter) needed to solve all kinds of problems are seen as involving an *interaction* of 'conceptual' and 'procedural' understanding. It should be noted that the model does *not* imply that these two types of understanding are mutually exclusive. Furthermore, other factors such as motivation, context or the pupil's perceived expectation of what should be

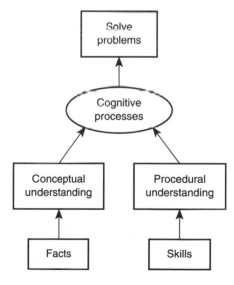

Fig. 2.1 A model for science (based on Gott and Mashiter, 1991)

done in a science lesson, each of which can have a significant effect on performance, are omitted.

For the implications of the model to be clear, we need first to define the terms used within it.

Solving problems

We indicated at the beginning of this section that the model is not confined exclusively to practical science. To retain this position, we need to adopt a very catholic definition of 'problem' to include any activity that requires a pupil to apply his or her understanding in a new situation. This will include explanation of phenomena, applied science problems, theoretical problems as well as what we will define as investigations. What differs between these is the relative emphasis on conceptual and procedural understanding.

This book, however, focuses primarily on investigative work which is one type of problem-solving and which is usually, but not exclusively, practical in nature.

Conceptual understanding and facts

Williams and Haladyna (1982) define facts as 'associations between names, other symbols, objects and locations', and concepts as 'classes of objects or events that are grouped together by virtue of sharing common defining attributes'. In the model, conceptual understanding refers to the understanding of the ideas in science which are based on facts, laws and principles and which are sometimes referred to as 'substantive' or 'declarative' concepts. We shall refer to these concepts as substantive concepts in the chapters that follow. Examples include energy, the laws of motion, heredity, solubility, photosynthesis and so on.

Procedural understanding and skills

Skills here refer to activities such as the use of measuring instruments and the construction of tables and graphs, which are necessary but not sufficient in themselves to the carrying out of most practical work. We will restrict the term to those mechanical aspects of these activities which we hope pupils will acquire and store in the background, so to speak, ready to be extracted as a tool, complete with in-built instructions for use.

Procedural understanding is the understanding of a set of ideas which is complementary to conceptual understanding but related to the 'knowing how' of science and concerned with the understanding needed to put science into practice. It is *the thinking behind the doing*. For example, in measurement in a plant growth study, procedural understanding does not refer to the measuring itself, but to the decisions that have to be made about what to measure, how often and over what time period. It also includes the understanding of the notion of the fair test as well as the nature of a line graph, how it differs from a bar chart or how it illustrates patterns between variables.

The content of procedural understanding is not well documented. Too often it is regarded solely as a means of acquiring a concept. Although procedural understanding *can* be a means of learning or learning about a concept, it is also a kind of understanding *in its own right*. The significance of procedural understanding underlies much of the argument in this book.

The term 'procedural knowledge' (or procedural understanding) is used in both maths and English but in a somewhat different sense. In maths, for instance, it relates to the use of problem-solving strategies; in English, to the construction of prose. In both these subjects, the procedural knowledge required is basically the recall and use of a set of rules (in maths, formulae or theories). In science, there is the additional problem of not only knowing the 'rules' (of the fair test for instance), but of relating these rules and the concepts of science to objective evidence. Similarly in history, reasons for or explanations of change need to be supported by some kind of evidence from primary or secondary sources. It is this collection and verification of data which can be seen as one distinguishing factor between procedural knowledge in science and history, and in other subjects.

Cognitive processes

Conceptual and procedural understanding cannot be totally independent of one another: some understanding of substantive concepts is necessary to carry out most procedural aspects of science, and similarly procedural understanding is necessary to put substantive concepts into practice. The cognitive processes in Fig. 2.1 refer to this interaction involving the selection and application of facts, skills, conceptual *and* procedural understanding. These cognitive processes are the means of obtaining or processing the information needed to tackle a problem successfully. Although procedural and conceptual understanding are intertwined in this way, the distinction between them is a useful one in unravelling the complexities of school science.

The emphasis of a particular task may be more on one side of the model than the other. Hence when the conceptual understanding required to solve a problem is very hard and the procedural understanding easy, then the balance is to the left and vice versa.

An example will serve to illustrate how the model we have put forward can be applied. Suppose that the problem is to find out how the average or final speed of a toy car travelling down a ramp is related to its weight. The pupil first needs to understand the concept of speed and know that it involves distance and time (*conceptual understanding*). He or she will need to have the *skills* to be able to measure distance, time and weight. Then the pupil must decide how to construct a fair test and what distance and time to measure (*procedural understanding*). All this information has to be *processed* in designing the investigation, examining the resulting data and drawing appropriate inferences, provided that the pupil considers that the data are 'believable' (*procedural understanding*).

An analogy may be useful here. The facts, skills and understandings can be envisaged as information or patterns in the brain's memory bank. When faced with a problem of any sort, but in the sense of some new experience which requires resolution, the brain can be imagined to scan its data banks

for facts or previous experiences that may help with the new problem. In the above example, those 'hard disk stores' will contain ideas about speed, measurement of distance and time, skill routines about using instruments, notions of a fair test and how it relates to the validity of any resulting data and so on. The central processing unit will then examine the problem and look on the hard disk for help; this may be in the form of particular ideas, or past experiences in similar circumstances. These will be pulled into the working memory. Then they must be 'processed', via a series of thought patterns that we label hypothesising, or predicting or whatever, into a solution consonant with, and evaluated against, the demands of the original problem. The 'processes' discussed in the previous chapter can now, by and large, be identified with these patterns of thought. Hypothesising, or predicting, or interpreting, or explaining are different operations of this central processing unit; different guides to the scanning of the memory banks of conceptual and procedural understanding.

We will argue that procedural understanding has to be *taught* in order that there is something in the relevant data stores for the central processor to access and structure.

Classifying practical work

We can use this model as a way of locating the trends and themes in science which we described in the last chapter. Armstrong's heurism, for instance, would lie firmly on the right-hand side of the model, while the reality of the Nuffield schemes emphasised the left-hand side. Duggan and Gott (1993) provide a useful summary which relates the five broad types of practical work put forward in the last chapter to their principal learning outcomes in terms of conceptual and procedural understanding (Table 2.1).

Table 2.1 demonstrates that each type of practical work has a significant role to play in practical science. While most types of practical work involve some elements of procedural and conceptual understanding, the table refers only to the *principal* learning outcome of each type. Hence, it could be

Table 2.1 Classification of types of practical work by their learning outcome (Duggan and Gott, 1994)

	Principal learning outcome	
Type of practical	*Conceptual understanding*	*Procedural understanding*
Skills		(skill) acquisition
Observation	application	
Enquiry	acquisition	
Illustration	consolidation	
Investigation	application	application and synthesis

argued that enquiry practicals could embody both conceptual and procedural understanding. That is certainly true in that there will be skills or data interpretation involved, but it is not the main purpose of the exercise. It could also be argued that if the aim is to acquire a concept, then asking pupils to deploy skills and procedural understanding *as well* may be inefficient. Experience of Nuffield and in the classroom suggests that such activities overload most pupils to the extent that none of the learning outcomes may be achieved.

Table 2.1 also shows the place of investigations in practical science in that they are the only type of practical work whose *principal* learning outcome is to provide pupils with the opportunity to achieve a thorough grasp of procedural understanding, while at the same time allowing pupils to use and refine their conceptual understanding. We shall return to this point again later.

Developing the model

In the last section, we used the model in Fig. 2.1 to describe two kinds of understanding that underpin science – conceptual and procedural understanding. In this section, we shall try to identify in greater detail the types and levels of conceptual and, particularly, procedural understanding that children need in science. In order to do this, we have used a taxonomy based on work by Bloom *et al.* (1956), which was originally intended for use in the American Grade System.

Bloom's taxonomy as a descriptor of science

Bloom's taxonomy of 'educational objectives for the cognitive domain' has been used, reused and modified to suit a wide variety of purposes. It was originally intended for assessment purposes to enable teachers to relate educational objectives in terms of subject content to the thinking processes involved. Williams and Haladyna (1982) write: 'The taxonomy is undoubtedly one of the most important contributions to educational practice in recent times. It was enthusiastically received and has been widely used ever since its publication.'

Kempa (1986) suggests that Nuffield O level science was based largely on the work of Bloom *et al.* He describes how Bloom's original taxonomy contains six different levels of cognitive ability which are hierarchical, in the sense that higher levels subsume lower levels. He continues: 'but for most science examinations three of these tend to be combined, giving a four level classification'. Kempa defines these four levels as:

- *Knowledge and recall* of scientific facts, hypotheses, theories and concepts, as well as terminology and convention.
- *Understanding* of scientific knowledge and relationships, which manifests itself in the student's ability to explain and interpret information presented, and to express it in alternative communication modes.
- *Application* of scientific knowledge and understanding to unfamiliar (i.e. novel) situations.

The ability to apply knowledge implies that the student is able to select from his or her knowledge reservoir those items of knowledge and relationships that are relevant to the novel situation.

- *Analysis, synthesis and evaluation* of scientific information, which involves the breaking down of information into its constituent parts (analysis) and reorganising it so that a new structure emerges (synthesis). Additionally, the information may have to be evaluated in terms of its validity or underlying assumptions, and consequences.

The difference therefore between understanding and application is that understanding is manifested within one context, whereas application is the ability to apply that understanding to other contexts.

The hierarchical structure of these taxonomies derived from Bloom has caused much distrust because it is difficult to relate to real situations. For instance, it is often difficult to distinguish between recall and understanding. There are also instances where evidence appears not to support the taxonomy. For example, it is relatively easy to create a practical situation in which a pupil will apply an idea that he or she is quite unable to recall, or see the relevance of, when faced with an apparently simple question. The 'simple' question may introduce a different context or style which causes the pupil difficulty. Nevertheless, the taxonomy can be used as a way of *describing* what science might contain, without getting into the complexities of whether or not it is possible to use the hierarchical structure to predict levels of difficulty.

We can apply this taxonomy to both types of understanding which we have defined above and used in the model in Fig. 2.1. To begin with, we shall describe briefly its application to the familiar concepts of science so that we can then demonstrate that a parallel structure for procedural understanding can be defined. We shall look at this less familiar structure in greater detail.

Bloom's taxonomy and conceptual understanding

We have simplified the classification above and applied it specifically to conceptual understanding:

Conceptual taxonomy

- Knowledge and recall of facts
- Understanding of concepts
- Application of concepts (in unfamiliar situations)
- Synthesis of concepts (in problem-solving).

As we noted above, we intend to use this taxonomy as a *description*, with no implications that it is a hierarchical structure. As a description of the science curriculum – one of many possible ones of course – it suggests that there will be a place for the simple recall of some parsimonious selection of facts. There must also be room for an understanding of the ideas, how the facts interrelate in the context in which they were taught, as well as the application of those ideas in novel situations. And, finally, in the context of solving problems, pupils must synthesise knowledge and conceptual understanding.

One of the weaknesses of the model here is that concepts can become more like facts with increasing age and experience. For instance, distance can be a concept in one situation to a young child but will be recalled and used much like a fact in another situation by an older pupil. So, as with all models, if it is pursued too far, it is in danger of collapse. That does not mean that it cannot help us as a descriptive tool in making some overall sense of the complexities inherent in the cognitive abilities required in science.

Bloom's taxonomy and procedural understanding

We can also use the taxonomy to explore the notion that the 'content' of the procedural aspects of science merits a similar differentiated treatment (Fig. 2.2).

We have based the procedural taxonomy on skills and 'concepts of evidence' which are complementary to the facts and substantive concepts occurring in the conceptual taxonomy of the previous section. Before we look at the structure of the taxonomy, however, it is important to clarify what we mean by 'concepts of evidence'.

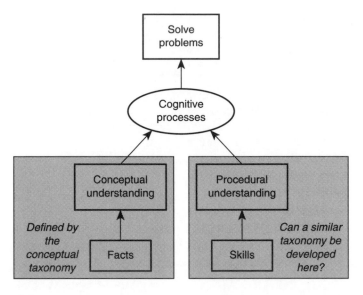

Fig. 2.2 Developing the model

Concepts of evidence

We have coined the phrase 'concepts of evidence', which we have used elsewhere (Duggan and Gott, 1994) to refer to the concepts which are associated with procedural understanding. In passing, we admit to having some doubt about this phrase. We have considered alternatives such as 'procedures', 'working methods' or 'procedural concepts', but none of these terms conveys the desired meaning: procedures or working methods tend to imply a low or algorithmic level of cognitive skill; procedural concepts again restricts the meaning to individual procedures and is somewhat confusing. Our term, concepts of evidence, draws attention to the importance of this understanding and the concepts underlying the doing of science in relation to the evidence as a whole.

Figure 2.3 shows how we have structured these concepts of evidence around the four main stages of investigative work: namely, those concepts associated with the design of the task, measurement, data handling and, finally but crucially, the evaluation of the complete task in terms of the reliability and validity of the ensuing evidence. By stages, we do not mean stages in time, since these stages are often revisited. For instance, at the data

handling stage, a decision may be made to take more measurements. The evaluation of the task requires an understanding of all three stages – design, measurement and data handling – and this understanding of evaluation is needed as much at the beginning as at the end of the task. The kind of understanding associated with each of these main stages is defined in detail in Table 2.2.

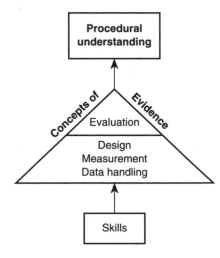

Fig. 2.3 Procedural understanding and concepts of evidence

Table 2.2 Concepts of evidence and their definition

Concepts of evidence		Definition
Associated with design	Variable identification	Understanding the idea of a variable and identifying the relevant variable to change (the independent variable) and to measure, or assess if qualitative (the dependent variable)
	Fair test	Understanding the structure of the fair test in terms of controlling the necessary variables and its importance in relation to the validity of any resulting evidence
	Sample size	Understanding the significance of an appropriate sample size to allow, for instance, for probability or biological variation
	Variable types	Understanding the distinction between categoric, discrete, continuous and derived variables and how they link to different graph types
Associated with measurement	Relative scale	Understanding the need to choose sensible values for quantities so that resulting measurements will be meaningful. For instance, a large quantity of chemical in a small quantity of water causing saturation, will lead to difficulty in differentiating the dissolving times of different chemicals
	Range and interval	Understanding the need to select a sensible range of values of the variables within the task so that the resulting line graph consists of values which are spread sufficiently widely and reasonably spaced out so that the 'whole' pattern can be seen. A suitable number of readings is therefore also subsumed in this concept
	Choice of instrument	Understanding the relationship between the choice of instrument and the required scale, range of readings required, and their interval (spread) and accuracy
	Repeatability	Understanding that the inherent variability in any physical measurement requires a consideration of the need for repeats, if necessary, to give reliable data
	Accuracy	Understanding the appropriate degree of accuracy that is required to provide reliable data which will allow a meaningful interpretation
Associated with data handling	Tables	Understanding that tables are more than ways of presenting data after they have been collected. They can be used as ways of organising the design and subsequent data collection and analysis in advance of the whole experiment.
	Graph type	Understanding that there is a close link between graphical representations and the type of variable they are to represent. For example, a categoric independent variable such as type of surface, cannot be displayed sensibly in a line graph. The behaviour of a continuous variable, on the other hand, is best shown in a line graph
	Patterns	Understanding that patterns represent the behaviour of variables and that they can be seen in tables and graphs
	Multivariate data	Understanding the nature of multivariate data and how particular variables within those data can be held constant to discover the effect of one variable on another
Associated with the evaluation of the complete task	**Reliability**	Understanding the implications of the measurement strategy for the reliability of the resulting data; can the data be believed?
	Validity	Understanding the implications of the design for the validity of the resulting data; an overall view of the task to check that it can answer the question

Car	Distance 1	Distance 2	Distance 3	Average
Blue				
Red				
Green				

We have used the term 'variable' in Table 2.2 to refer to any observation which can be described by different values – for example, temperature, length or time. Variables can be classified in terms of their roles and functions in the structure of the activity as 'independent', 'dependent' or 'control' variables.

The values for the 'independent' variable are chosen and manipulated by the investigator. The value of the 'dependent' variable is then measured for each change in value of the independent variable. 'Control' variables are those which must be kept constant while the independent variable is changed to make the test 'fair'. Many scientific tasks can be defined in this way according to their 'variable structure'. For example, supposing the task is to find the effect of car colour on frequency of accidents, the car colour is the *independent* variable, the frequency of accidents is the *dependent* variable and the age of the driver is one of several *control* variables. These terms are used in the National Curriculum of the UK. We should note here that we are conscious of the limitations of defining procedural understanding in terms of the variable structure of a task, a point to which we shall return.

It is important to note that concepts of measurement are to do with the decisions that have to be made about measurement rather than to do with the *skill* of measurement itself. For instance, in a task about the effect of temperature on the dissolving time of sugar, it is not the ability of the pupil to use a thermometer (which we define as a skill), but rather the decisions that he or she has

taken about, for example, the range and interval of temperatures and the number of repeats which reflect the understanding that the pupil has about these particular concepts of measurement.

Concepts associated with data handling include the understanding of the use of a table as a way of organising data rather than the construction of tables themselves. Hence *before even beginning measurement*, a pupil may construct a table of values of the variable which he or she is going to change. For instance, in the dissolving example to which we have already referred, the pupil may construct a table with temperatures of 25, 50, 75 and 100°C before beginning the task. Or for the task of finding out the distance travelled by different coloured toy cars, the pupil may construct a table such as the one above.

A further aspect of data handling is the isolation of the required variable from multivariate data. For example, in the multivariate table below, to consider the effect of temperature it is necessary to compare the times in the left-hand column with those in the right-hand column. Alternatively, to consider the relative dissolving times of caster and brown sugar, the times in the top row have to be compared with those in the bottom row.

	Hot	Cold
Caster sugar	(sec)	(sec)
Brown sugar	(sec)	(sec)

The final evaluation stage subsumes all the other concepts of evidence because reliability and validity can only be considered in the context of the strategy of the whole task.

There are other ideas that could, and perhaps should, be included in this list. For example, the notion of ratio and proportionality is much used in science. On what grounds are they excluded when the concept of 'patterns' is included? The obvious but not wholly convincing answer, is that patterns, which are in the list, must include ratio and proportionality. The other argument is that proportionality and ratio are mathematical ideas within the basic (or axiomatic) construction of mathematics. We have attempted to restrict our definition of concepts of evidence to ideas that relate data to reality, which is a crucial distinction between mathematics (which only needs to be self-consistent) and science (which has to satisfy the requirements of the behaviour of objects in the real world).

The significance of evidence and the notion of audience

We shall see later, if we take the evaluation of a task as an indicator, that the notion of data as evidence would appear to be understood by very few pupils. The model we have developed is based on the assumption that evidence is an important notion in science education. It might be useful here to stand back for a moment and ask *why* we believe evidence to be important?

If we adopt the view that the aim of science is simply to arrive at a set of concepts which can explain real-life behaviour, we can then test this theory against some actual examples. If we consider universal gravitation, for instance, then the substantive concept of gravity can explain this phenomenon successfully. Evidence here takes a secondary role in the real world of school science in that it serves only to validate what is now accepted theory, although at the time the theory was being established, evidence was crucial for its validation. If we consider the phenomenon of elas-

ticity, then we can use Hooke's Law to explain stretching reasonably well, although the relationship varies with different materials and the law is only applicable within certain limits. In this example, sound evidence is crucial because data are required to make the law usable – a spring constant needs to be calculated for specific instances. Finally, if we consider the rate of water flow in a river, this is extremely difficult to explain without empirical evidence (perhaps aided by computer modelling). Here, the data are the basis for the model and are paramount. This is not to say, of course, that substantive concepts do not guide the model; for instance, the concept of friction will suggest that the flow may be less at particular locations. In these three examples, evidence and the data which supports it are important but they take on different roles from validating theory in the first example to being the key component in the last. Similarly, the conceptual element is crucial in the first example but of less importance in the last.

In all three examples above, the evidence is needed to justify the outcome. In the first example, however, the theory of universal gravitation is so well accepted that evidence which supports the theory is unlikely to be closely scrutinised, particularly in the classroom. It could of course be argued that this should not be the case; theoretically, evidence should always be important. In reality, however, if the lesson is about illustrating Boyle's Law, then as long as the evidence broadly supports the theory, it is likely to be accepted without question. The chances of refuting a long-established substantive concept in the school laboratory are indeed low. However, in the third example the evidence determines the model, so it is open to interpretation and indeed to misinterpretation. Because the 'solution' is not obvious, the evidence is much more crucial. If the model is to be believed, it must be supported by sound evidence. In science, it is often necessary to make that evidence public or available for others to see, so that they can evaluate for themselves how much weight to give to the explanation, interpretation or solution.

If we can get across this sense of the public

nature of evidence or, to put it another way, the idea of evidence for an audience, then pupils are more likely to understand the notion of data as evidence. We shall return to the notion of audience in Chapter 6 when we consider strategies for introducing these ideas in the classroom or laboratory.

We have introduced these ideas here because the significance of evidence (and of concepts of evidence) in science underlies our views of procedural understanding, to which we shall now return.

A procedural taxonomy

We have developed a taxonomy for procedural understanding which is shown below using skills and concepts of evidence:

Procedural taxonomy

- Knowledge and recall of skills
- Understanding of concepts of evidence
- Application of concepts of evidence (in unfamiliar situations)
- Synthesis of skills and concepts of evidence (in problem-solving)

Some examples may help to show how the taxonomy might be applied. As with the conceptual version discussed earlier, we are suggesting here that a curriculum should contain something of the knowledge and recall of skills, such as the use of a thermometer. It should also encompass the understanding of concepts of evidence, as in the understanding of the role of the fair test within a familiar context, or the range and number of readings required in measurements of temperature. The concepts must also be applied to novel situations (transferred). The ability to apply the notion of the fair test should be available in a whole range of circumstances: in all experimental work of whatever type, or in criticism of other people's experimental accounts. Finally, we have the ability to synthesise skills and concepts of evidence into the solution to a problem where, for instance, the links between a

fair test and the validity of any resulting data, or between the accuracy of a set of readings and the reliability of the data, are taken into account in generating 'believable' data.

We can see, therefore, that the descriptive model which has been so influential in structuring and assessing the conceptual component of the science curriculum can also be applied in a similar way to the procedural component. The importance of this is not in some arbitrary mirroring of an existing structure or imposing a needless level of complexity on an already complex enough situation. Rather, it is to do with recognising that there is a *content* to the procedural side of science which can be described and which must be recognised and planned for in curriculum design and assessment.

If we reconsider the principal learning outcome of the main categories of practical work which we put forward earlier in the light of these two taxonomies, we can see that observation practicals are mainly about the application and synthesis of conceptual understanding. Illustrative practicals usually concern the understanding of substantive concepts. Investigations, however, provide the opportunity for pupils to synthesise conceptual and procedural understanding.

An alternative perspective of the relationship between concepts of evidence and the science curriculum that deserves mention is the psychological perspective, which is exemplified by the thinking skills movement.

The thinking skills approach and CASE

There is a growing movement towards the teaching of 'higher-order' thinking skills in the UK (Young, 1993) and a recognition that such teaching has a valuable contribution to make to the curriculum (see, for example, Coles and Robinson, 1989). 'Higher order here' refers to the thinking which is not tied to specific subjects and includes, for example, the ability to sort out common features or patterns in a series of pictures or texts or to generalise from them. It also includes the ability to evaluate conflicting evidence. There are several courses, all of which are based on the notion of flexible and articulate thinking. Children are encouraged to think about their own thinking (*metacognition*) and to reflect and share their learning experiences. The teacher is seen as a mediator and facilitator.

These courses stem from a psychological perspective and are based largely on the work of Piaget and Vygotsky. Many are not specifically science-based. The Somerset Thinking Skills course (Blagg *et al.*, 1988), for instance, is usually set within English or Personal and Social Education (PSE) lessons. It uses visual activities and focuses on categories of thinking which include recognising patterns, dealing in probabilities, drawing analogies, evaluation, analysis and synthesis. Another course, Feuerstein's Instrumental Enrichment programme, is based on Vygotsky's theory that every human being has the potential to become an effective learner. The teacher by mediation can promote the child's cognitive development.

The Cognitive Acceleration through Science Education (CASE; Adey *et al.*, 1989) intervention is, however, set within science lessons, and like the Somerset course, emphasises the importance of transfer and of metacognition. The CASE project is based on the argument that the science curriculum makes high cognitive demands on average secondary school pupils which are not adequately dealt with in 'normal' teaching. This 'mismatch' is addressed by an intervention which is aimed at improving or accelerating the child's reasoning processes. These same reasoning processes are particularly relevant in practical science. The theory behind the method stems from Piagetian psychology, which is outlined briefly below.

Piaget's developmental model

In *The Growth of Logical Thinking from Childhood to Adolescence*, Inhelder and Piaget (1958) report the findings of detailed studies of the growth of mathematical and scientific concepts in children. This book was a landmark in the history of psychological investigation into thinking and reasoning processes. It had (and to some extent still has) a profound influence on psychology and education. It has to be said, however, that Piaget was first and foremost a psychologist and epistemologist. His developmental model and his experiments were intended to be diagnostic tools for classifying children's thinking processes and were not intended to be transferred directly to the classroom.

Piaget's developmental model is based on the idea that the child's thinking progresses through a number of stages (Fig. 2.4), each of which follows on from the successful acquisition of the previous stage. There are three fundamental stages – the sensori-motor stage (approximately the first 18 months of life), the concrete operational stage (up to about 12 years) and the formal operational stage (12–15 years) – the last two being most relevant to primary and secondary education. Each of these stages has sub-periods and sub-stages. The concrete operational stage, for instance, has two sub-periods: the pre-operational sub-period (18 months to about 7 years) and the concrete operational sub-period (approximately 7 to 12 years). The kind of thinking which characterises each of these stages and more importantly the limitations of the thinking and reasoning at each stage, applies to the handling of all sorts of concepts right across the curriculum. The child's progress from one stage to another occurs through a process of *equilibration* – an interaction of cognitive growth and environmental input.

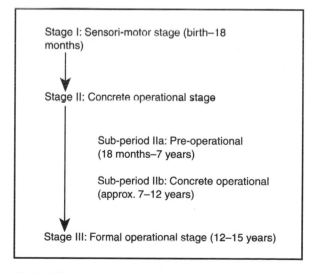

Stage I: Sensori-motor stage (birth–18 months)

Stage II: Concrete operational stage

Sub-period IIa: Pre-operational (18 months–7 years)

Sub-period IIb: Concrete operational (approx. 7–12 years)

Stage III: Formal operational stage (12–15 years)

Fig. 2.4 Piaget's developmental model

Piaget's evidence on formal reasoning came largely from fifteen experiments which were undertaken by children between the ages of 4 and 16. Each of these experiments consisted of a problem-solving task not unlike investigations, during which the subject was encouraged to experiment so that he or she could then explain certain phenomena to the observer. These tasks were used to explore the kind of thinking that the children were using to tackle the problem. The fourth of Piaget's experiments – 'the oscillation of a pendulum' – will serve to illustrate Piaget's theory and the relevance of this model both for the CASE project and for the framework we are developing.

In the pendulum experiment, the children were given string which could be shortened or lengthened and a set of varying weights and asked to find out what factor(s) affect the oscillation of the pendulum. The pre-operational child's thinking is characteristically *egocentric*, in that she regards the world from her own point of view, unaware that there are other points of view or that she is limited by her own. For instance, the pre-operational child will confirm her own theory regardless of the evidence and will often go on to contradict her own previous theories. In the case of the pendulum, she will be unable to isolate a particular variable such as weight. The concrete operational child will, however, be able to order length, weight, etc., and be able to make objective judgements, but will have difficulty isolating one variable in a multivariate situation – she may, for instance, alter string length and weight simultaneously. A child at this stage, then, has difficulty with the idea of controls and the concept of fair testing. The older child at the third stage (formal operations) will, according to Piaget's theory, manipulate one variable at a time and be able to look at several combinations of variables and then arrive at a valid conclusion.

Piaget's theory has been the subject of much criticism. The idea, for instance, that the stages are related to chronological age was soon overtaken by the view that they are more likely to be related to mental age (e.g. Dodwell, 1961). Similarly, the notion of the development of concepts across the curriculum being at the same cognitive stage simultaneously has been disputed (see, for example,

Annett, 1959). More fundamentally, the relationship of Piaget's theory to education has been the subject of much criticism (see Brown and Desforges, 1977; Rowell, 1984). His theory has been interpreted in a variety of ways, most of which have caused controversy. Rowell (1984) carries out a thorough and comprehensive review of the arguments for and against the import of psychological theory in education and points out some of the assumptions which underpin Piaget's theory. We shall not enter the debate, but in passing draw the reader's attention to the fact that the basis of the CASE project is not uncontroversial. We should note, however, that Piaget used the tasks as *indicators* of levels of thinking, as assessment tools, and as such they are not necessarily central to the issue – any appropriate tasks would do.

The CASE project

The CASE project (Adey, 1988, 1992; Adey and Shayer, 1990) used Piaget's theory to develop an intervention strategy in the early years of secondary school which is designed to accelerate the development of formal operational thinking. The intervention strategy focuses very specifically on activities designed to promote types of reasoning which are characteristic of the formal operational stage (Table 2.3). The CASE project uses a series of science activities, some of which are investigative in nature, allowing pupils an opportunity to 'test tentative theories against reality' because 'It is only by interaction with reality that a learner can test his/her models of the nature of reality' (Adey, 1992).

Table 2.3 The focus of the CASE activities

Control of variables
Proportionality
Compensation
Probability
Combinations
Correlation
Classification
Formal models
Compound variables
Equilibrium

The intervention consists of thirty activities which are designed to be used alongside the 'normal' science curriculum at the rate of about one a fortnight over a two-year period. The first activities focus on the relevant vocabulary (variables, etc.). Then each of the reasoning patterns which is thought to underlie formal operational thinking is taken in turn and a lesson built around it. The underlying premise is that science *requires* higher levels of cognitive thinking (see, for instance, the early work by Shayer (1972, 1974) on the Nuffield O level syllabus). So if Piagetian tasks can be used in reverse, so to speak, to accelerate cognitive development, then pupils will be better able to cope with science. Again the emphasis is not on the particular tasks so much as on the *type* of task that articulates with the pupil's developing logical structures.

Activity 3, for example, which follows two activities designed to introduce the idea of variables, is built around the idea of the fair test. Children are given a variety of lengths and widths of tubing in different materials and asked to investigate the effects of the variables (length and width) on the note produced when the tubes are blown across. The children are instructed to try the tubes in pairs and asked whether particular pairs of tubes provide fair tests. The method is prescribed, although the control of variables is not specifically stated. The pupils are given worksheets, which by providing a table with the variables as headings, direct the pupils towards repeating their readings and the method of recording and presenting their results. Pupils are then asked specific questions such as:

- What is the effect of *length*?
- Which experiments tell you this?
- What is the effect of *material*?
- Which experiments tell you this?

(Adey *et al.*, 1989)

In this way, they are directed towards making a generalisation or conclusion. The worksheet provided therefore quite tightly controls the activity in terms of the method, the questions to be answered, the format of the results and the conclusions drawn, and in this sense the activities are closed. A series of written fair test problems is provided as a follow-up to the practical.

We can compare this activity with a typical investigation (Fig. 2.5). The similarities are clear. Each task is concerned with the identification of the effects of more than one independent variable (material, length and width of the tubes; length and width of the beams). However, in the investigation, the problem is defined but the method is only limited in so far as the equipment is provided. The pupils can then decide how to use the equipment, what measurements to take, how many measurements to take and so on, so that the method and means of arriving at a solution are open. We shall return to the difference between the CASE activities and investigations later in the next section.

A decorating problem

Sally and Sam watched Mum and Dad decorating.
To reach a high place, Dad put a plank of wood between two chairs.

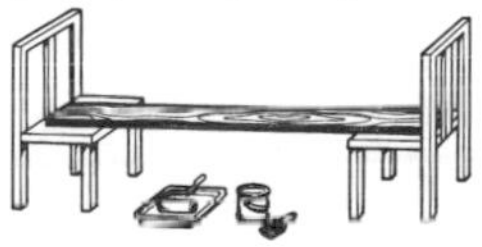

Mum said, 'The plank will bend too much. You're too heavy.'
Sally said, 'If you use a different plank, it won't bend as much.'
Sam said, 'If you use a wider plank, it won't bend as much.'

Who was right?

Find out whether the amount the wood bends depends on
(a)   the type of material which is used, or
(b)   the width of the material, or
(c)   both of these

Write a clear report saying what you did and what you found out. Don't forget to show your results.

Fig. 2.5 Example of an investigation (from Foulds *et al.*, 1992)

As well as the individual activities, there are three essential features in the teaching of CASE which we shall consider in turn: *cognitive conflict*, *metacognition* and *bridging*.

Cognitive conflict

Cognitive conflict refers to the situation in which a pupil is confronted by results which do not fit his or her existing expectations. The conflict means that the pupil may be forced to 'equilibrate' or reconstruct his or her thinking in order to accommodate the new evidence. Since conflict stimulates cognitive development, pupils are encouraged to acknowledge and consider conflict when it occurs. It is of course possible to avoid cognitive conflict by ignoring the results or by accommodating conflicting evidence.

Metacognition

Metacognition here refers to the process whereby the teacher encourages pupils to reflect on their own thinking processes. For instance, the class might discuss what aspects of an activity they found difficult and why.

Bridging

Bridging, the third feature of CASE teaching, is usually in the last part of the lesson when the teacher draws the pupils' attention to the use of the relevant reasoning pattern in completely different contexts, in science or elsewhere. Clearly, this feature is designed to promote transfer; that is, the transfer of learning from one situation to another, which we defined as *application* in an earlier section.

The CASE intervention strategy was first tried from 1984 to 1987 with pupils in years 7 and 8. Cognitive development was measured using the Piagetian Science Reasoning Test both before and after the intervention. The results suggested that immediately after the intervention, the experimental group of pupils showed significantly better levels of cognitive development than the control group, but no better performance in science in each school's end of year science tests. Two and three years after the intervention, however, the experimental group performed significantly better at GCSE in science as well as in mathematics and English. These early results are encouraging and have the potential to have a profound influence on education. There is, however, a need for large-scale replication, particularly since the size of the 1987 sample was limited. The subsequent analysis, while not denying the potential importance of the approach, has come in for some criticism (Preece, 1993). There is clearly a need for further empirical work on the effects of the CASE approach.

Concepts of evidence and CASE

What is the relationship between the psychological perspective of the CASE intervention and the taxonomic approach put forward in the first half of this chapter? Clearly, the CASE intervention has a much wider goal in that it aims to improve thinking skills in general which will be applicable in other subject areas. Our taxonomic approach is targeted much more specifically on science.

There are, however, similarities between the focus of some of the CASE activities and some concepts of evidence such as variables and probability. There are also areas which are not covered by the CASE approach and vice versa. The three essential features of CASE teaching (namely, cognitive conflict, bridging and metacognition), however, have much in common with well-taught investigative work, as we shall see in Chapters 6 and 7.

We have already noted that the CASE activities tend to be relatively closely controlled, whereas investigative tasks, which allow children the opportunity to apply and synthesise conceptual and procedural understanding, are 'open' in the sense of, for instance, allowing children to choose their own methods. The more fundamental differences between these two approaches are:

1 The CASE approach comes at the problem via an assumption that the intervention will accelerate cognitive development so that the pupil will be better equipped to do all of science as

well as other subjects. The taxonomic approach assumes that concepts of evidence are 'things that can be taught' as *part of science*, which will increase individuals' capacity to cope with problems simply because they know more about how to set about it as well as the ability to evaluate other people's evidence. Ultimately, the approach aims to improve procedural understanding.

2 Following the CASE intervention, pupils are expected to return to the teacher's 'normal' scheme of work, which may not include any further tasks which focus on concepts of evidence. The taxonomic approach suggests that concepts of evidence be gradually taught and developed through progressively more difficult tasks and then regularly practised and reinforced within investigations as part of the teacher's scheme of work.

3 The CASE approach focuses on individual concepts of evidence, whereas the taxonomic approach to procedural understanding aims to improve the understanding, *application and synthesis* of similar concepts by enabling pupils to carry out whole investigations and put their understanding into practice. Investigations, therefore, allow opportunities for pupils to demonstrate the highest level of cognitive ability.

We would argue that defining the science curriculum to include concepts of evidence is likely to be the more productive way of looking at the issue: its inclusion in the list of things to be taught and learnt would ensure its presence in the classroom so that procedural understanding is taught in its own right.

Summary

To arrive at a framework we have used a model and a classification based on Bloomian taxonomy, which have enabled us to locate the developments in practical science outlined in the last chapter and to describe in some detail the cognitive abilities which are inherent in sound practical science. While the taxonomy has its weaknesses which we

have discussed, it has been used here to help us unravel some of the complexities of 'doing' science. It has also enabled us to demonstrate that the levels of cognitive ability commonly used in relation to the conceptual component of science can be applied in a similar way to the procedural component. We have introduced the idea of concepts of evidence which will be used to structure the discussion of the data in forthcoming chapters. We hope that we have persuaded the reader that procedural understanding is more than a matter of recalling and using skills and procedures, but rather that it is a set of understandings which are important in their own right. This understanding is important not only in practical science but also as a means of effectively examining evidence from other sources.

The CASE intervention which adopts a psychological perspective has been considered as an alternative way of teaching concepts of evidence. While both approaches teach concepts of evidence, one of the key differences is that the psychological approach of the CASE intervention is aimed at increasing the scientific reasoning ability through a series of tasks which then, in principle at least, become redundant. The taxonomic approach to procedural understanding, on the other hand, aims at promoting the application and synthesis of concepts of evidence which are seen as a 'content' of the curriculum in their own right. Investigations provide the opportunity for pupils to put such ability into practice. In the next chapter, we shall look more closely at the definition of investigations.

References

Adey, P. (1988). Cognitive acceleration: Review and prospects. *International Journal of Science Education*, 10(2): 121–34.

Adey, P. (1992). The CASE results: Implications for science teaching. *International Journal of Science Education*, 14(2): 137–46.

Adey, P. and Shayer, M. (1990). Accelerating the development of formal thinking in middle and high school pupils. *Journal of Research in Science Teaching*, 27(6): 553–74.

Adey, P.S., Shayer, M. and Yates, C. (1989). *Thinking Science: The Materials of the CASE Project. Teacher's Pack*. London: MacMillian.

Adey, P.S., Shayer, M. and Yates, C. (1989). *Thinking Science: The Materials of the CASE Project Teacher's Pack.* London, Macmillan.

Annett, M. (1959). The classification of four common class concepts by children and adults. *British Journal of Educational Psychology*, 29: 223–35.

Blagg, N.R., Ballinger, M.P., Gardner, R.J., Petty, M. and Williams, G. (1988). *The Somerset Thinking Skills Course: Foundations for Problem-solving*. Oxford, Blackwell.

Bloom, B.S., Engelhart, M.D., Furst, E.J., Hill, W.H. and Krathwohl, D.R. (1956). *Taxonomy of Educational Objectives: The Cognitive Domain*. New York, Longmans, Green.

Brown, G. and Desforges, C. (1977). Piagetian psychology and education: Time for revision. *British Journal of Educational Psychology*, 47: 7–17.

Coles, M.J. and Robinson, W.D. (1989). *Teaching Thinking: A Survey of Programmes in Education*. Bristol, Classical Press.

Dodwell, P.C. (1961). Children's understanding of number concepts: Characteristics of an individual and a group test. *Canadian Journal of Psychology*, 15: 29–36.

Duggan, S. and Gott, R. (in press). The place of investigations in practical work in the UK National Curriculum for Science. *International Journal of Science Education*.

Foulds, K., Gott, R. and Feasey, R. (1992). 'Investigative Work in Science'. Unpublished research report, University of Durham.

Gott, R. and Mashiter, J. (1991). Practical work in science – a task-based approach? In: *Practical Science* (B.E. Woolnough, ed.). Buckingham, Open University Press.

Inhelder, B. and Piaget, J. (1958). *The Growth of Logical Thinking from Childhood to Adolescence: An Essay on the Construction of Formal Operational Structures*. London, Routledge and Kegan Paul.

Kempa, R. (1986). *Assessment in Science*. Cambridge Science Education Series. Cambridge, Cambridge University Press.

Preece, P.F.W. (1993). Comment: Cognitive acceleration and science achievement. *Journal of Research in Science Teaching*, 30(8): 1005–6.

Rowell, J.A. (1984). Many paths to knowledge: Piaget and science education. *Studies in Science Education*, 11: 1–25.

Shayer, M. (1972). Conceptual demands in Nuffield O level physics. *School Science Review*, 186(54): 26–34.

Shayer, M. (1974). Conceptual demands in the Nuffield O level biology course. *School Science Review*, 56(195): 381–8.

Williams, R.G. and Haladyna, T.M. (1982). Logical operations for generating intended questions (LOGIQ): A typology for higher level test items. In: *A Technology for Test-item Writing* (G.H. Roid and T.M. Haladyna, eds). London, Academic Press.

Young, S. (1993). Notching the brain cells up a gear. *Times Educational Supplement*, 12 February.

CHAPTER 3

Investigations: What are they?

In the last chapter, we developed a framework for practical science within which we located the role of investigations. But what qualifies as an investigation, and are there different types of investigations? Lack of clarity of definition has bedevilled (and still does bedevil) education in general, and science education in particular. In this chapter, we shall consider some major research projects which have concerned themselves with investigations and which have developed ways of classifying different types of investigations.

Problem-solving and investigations

There has been some confusion about the relationship between problem-solving and investigations which we shall consider here briefly. Problem-solving is a general term which has been applied to many subject areas. In maths and science, for instance, it has frequently been applied to cognitive, written problems. Its place in science education has been reviewed by Garrett (1986), who ends his paper: 'As Sham (1976) has pointed out, the whole field of endeavour in problem-solving is particularly vast and largely disorganised and this has been shown to be true even in the limited area of science education.'

Watts and Gilbert (1989) have attempted to classify problem-solving in science into two kinds of tasks: first, the paper and pencil tasks which are well defined and have little or no redundant infor-mation. Watts and Gilbert call these PS1 tasks. PS1 tasks were particularly prevalent in the 1970s and mid-1980s. Second, there are the wide variety of 'ill-defined' problem-solving tasks which emerged in the late 1980s, called PS2 tasks. By ill-defined they mean here tasks 'where only outline relevant information and materials are supplied' (Watts and Gilbert, 1989). Watts and Gilbert suggest that PS2 tasks have grown out of the search for a means of making science relevant and of allowing pupils to apply scientific principles. These tasks can be either written or practical but have a strong emphasis on skills and methods and include puzzles, design-and-make activities, and extended project work. Investigations can be seen as one type of problem-solving, in science, whose definition we shall now consider.

The Assessment of Performance Unit

The Assessment of Performance Unit (APU) was set up by the Department of Education and Science (DES) following political debates in the 1970s which expressed concern about standards in education. Its brief was wide-ranging and considerable funds were made available for an innovative approach to assessment. The intention was that a number of subjects, including maths, science and English, would be assessed using a 'light sampling' process. The light sampling process allows tests to be created which are much longer than could be taken by any individual pupils. These extended tests, in which several papers were produced and given to different, but parallel, samples of pupils, the results then being aggregated, provided the opportunity for a wide-ranging review of what constituted science in schools at that time. Hence, although no pupil was tested for more than an hour, the composite results were equivalent to a test lasting as long as 19 hours. Pupils in both primary and secondary schools in England and Wales at the ages of 11, 13 and 15 were sampled. The assessment was based on a framework comprising six science activity categories (SACs). It should be noted that the APU used the term science 'activity' rather than 'process', which suggests mental process. Their work focused, it claimed, on the assessment of the 'doing' of science rather than on cognitive processes. The six activity categories were:

1 Using symbolic representation.
2 Using apparatus and measuring instruments.
3 Observation tasks.
4 Interpretation and application.
5 Planning of investigations.
6 Performing investigations.   (APU, 1985)

It is with the last category, the performance of investigations, that we are concerned here.

The APU defined an investigation as 'a task for which the pupil cannot immediately see an answer or recall a routine method for finding it'. The APU recognised that this type of practical work was different from other types of practical work. Hence, a report in 1989 stated that: '"Performing investigations" enjoyed a unique status in that it was perceived and justified as the embodiment of an important aim of science teaching which encompasses more than the separate elements represented in the other Categories, all of which are involved in it' (APU, 1989).

The types of task defined as investigations by the APU (1987) and an example of each are shown in Table 3.1. In practice, the constraints of the national assessment (e.g. time and cost of equipment) limited the number of types of tasks that could be used. The last three types in Table 3.1 were developed and trialled, but not used in large-scale surveys. The initial aim was to select investigations within these two types which did not rely heavily on concepts. In that way, it was possible to assess a single facet of pupil performance – procedural understanding. Some of the investigations used are shown in Table 3.2.

The first four of these investigations are of the 'decide which...' type and the rest are of the 'find the effect of...' type. It will be seen that the investigations span a wide range of 'contexts'. Context here refers to the wording in which the investigation is embedded. In the main, the investigations are set in an 'everyday' (familiar) as opposed to a 'scientific' context, and they vary in the degree to which the question is defined. 'Swingboard', for instance, defines the variables to be tested (i.e. length and width), while 'Flooring' is entirely open since the pupil has to decide what 'suitable' means. The children were given equipment from which to choose, but other than this their choice of method was entirely open. Children were observed individually while performing investigations. The emphasis on

Table 3.1 The types of questions defined by the APU as investigations

Problem type	Example
Decide which...	...kind of paper towel will hold the most water.
Find the effect of...	...the water level in a container on the rate at which the water runs out of a hole in the bottom.
Find a way to...	...adapt weighing scales that won't measure up to the baggage allowance.
Find the cause of...	...the failure of a light bulb to light a circuit.
Make a structure/machine to...	...support a brick using one newspaper and sellotape.

Table 3.2 The APU (1985) investigations

Question title	Investigation
Survival	Which fabric would keep you warmer? (given 2 fabrics)
Cars	If all the cars are given the same chance, which one will travel furthest? (given 3 cars)
Paper towel	Which kind of paper will hold the most water? (given 3 kinds)
Flooring	Which one of the floor coverings do you think is the most suitable for a kitchen floor? (given 4 types)
Woodlice	If woodlice are given a choice of the four places below, which one do they choose to lie in? A place which is: damp and dark, dry and dark, damp and light, or dry and light?
Hotwash	Does this washing powder wash a dirty cloth as clean in cold water as it does in hot water?
Candle	How does the angle of a wax taper affect its rate of burning?
Swingboard	What difference does changing the length and width of the board make to how quickly it swings?

procedures was accompanied by a growing awareness of the importance of variables in investigations in defining their difficulty.

A descriptive model (Fig. 3.1) was developed by the APU teams primarily to consider those aspects of performance which it was thought appropriate to assess. The model provides a more detailed description of what is going on when pupils perform investigations. This model is not supposed to represent the mental processes that pupils must go through in order to carry out an investigation, but rather it is a list of things that can be done, not necessarily in that order and not necessarily doing all of them. The intention behind the model was to describe an iterative approach, with the investigator continually evaluating decisions and adjusting as necessary. The first cycle around the loop might, for instance, be nothing more than a trial run to get the 'feel' of the quantities involved.

The APU data had considerable impact in schools. While at first it was seen as a threat to school autonomy, it was later seen to have developed innovative techniques which worked well in the classroom as curriculum material rather than merely as assessment items. In particular, the investigations were found to be of considerable interest to pupils in terms of enjoyment.

We shall discuss the findings of the APU research in detail in the next chapter.

Skills, concepts of evidence and the APU problem-solving model

The problem-solving model used by the APU has been used widely in science and indeed in other subjects. The factors itemised in the model encompass the skills and concepts of evidence defined in Chapter 2. The understanding which guides the ongoing evaluation, the iterative loops, are, in terms of concepts of evidence, equivalent to the notions of validity and reliability. This continuous reflection on the design and implementation in the light of the problem as set and the requirement of the data to answer it is, as we shall see later, the single most important factor missing in pupils' work, in all investigations and at all ages.

The Open-ended work in Science (OPENS) project

The OPENS project was a three-year research project also set up by the Department of Education and Science, to explore how open work can best be incorporated into science curricula and how it can be assessed. It was divided into two phases. The first phase reviewed the understanding and practice of open work among teachers of years 7–11 in secondary schools (Simon and Jones, 1992) while the second phase used this knowledge to test out the development of open work in schools (Jones et al., 1992). The project defined 'open

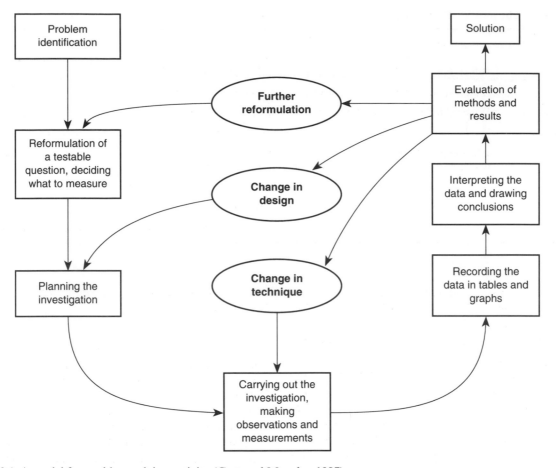

Fig. 3.1 A model for problem-solving activity (Gott and Murphy, 1987)

work' as 'activities which give the initiative to students for finding the solution to problems. These activities place an emphasis on autonomy in making decisions and on the integration of knowledge and skills' (Simon and Jones, 1992).

The project reviewed what teachers of years 7–11 mean by open activities and found that the term is used to refer to a wide variety of tasks including investigations, but also extending to project work, model-making and surveys. In order to classify these tasks according to their degree of openness, Simon and Jones suggest that three stages in the 'doing' of the activity need to be considered: defining the problem, choosing the method and arriving at a solution (Fig. 3.2). The first two stages in any task can be positioned on a

continuum ranging from 'closely defined' to 'not defined'. The last stage, arriving at a solution, can be positioned on a similar continuum ranging from activities where there is only one solution to those where there are many possible solutions (for example, a survey). Clearly, tasks considered to be *open* lie to the right of the continuum in one or more of their stages.

This framework was developed to enable teachers to see how they could manipulate the degree of openness in tasks, which in turn depends on what they want their pupils to learn. Simon and Jones point out that moving the stage of a task from left to right on the continuum generally results in moving the initiative from the teacher to the pupils.

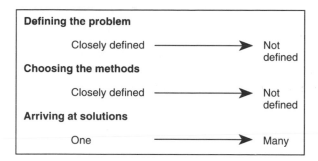

Fig. 3.2 The OPENS continua (based on Simon and Jones, 1992)

Returning to the definition of investigations arrived at in the previous chapter, we would suggest that activities that lie to the extreme closed end of each of the three continua, cannot qualify as investigations since they severely limit the opportunity for pupils to use and apply procedural understanding. On the classification developed in the previous chapters, activities of this kind might fall into the categories of enquiry or illustrative practicals. Some examples of tasks and how they might be crudely classified on the extremes of the continua are given in Table 3.3.

Task 1 in Table 3.3 is a closed task on all the continua and qualifies as an enquiry-based practical in that it is carefully structured to enable all pupils to reach the same endpoint. Task 2 is an investigation, since although the task defines the dependent variable (the number of seeds that germinate), it is otherwise open in that the method is chosen by the pupil and the solution could be one of many. Task 3 is clearly an open task on all three continua. If the investigations used in the APU survey and those used in the research to be reported here are classified using the OPENS framework, it becomes clear that in the 'defining the problem' stage, the investigations fall largely at the 'closely defined' end. The tasks given to the pupils were determined by the teacher/researcher, while choosing methods and arriving at solutions were open. The 'defining the problem' stage was closed for pragmatic reasons. To compare performance in research terms, pupils had to be given the same tasks, otherwise there would have been no effective control of the task they actually carried out.

The examples overleaf drawn from our research show how somewhat different methods can emerge when groups of pupils are presented with the same task.

Here we can see that Ross and Kevin designed their investigation so that the weight required to make the bridge sag by 10 cm was the dependent variable, while in Simon and Gavin's design, the sag of the bridge with 150 g weight was the dependent variable.

Table 3.3 Classifying tasks on the OPENS continua

1 Put 20 seeds on the windowsill and 20 seeds in a dark cupboard. Leave them for 10 days. Count how many seeds germinate in each batch.

2 How does the amount of light affect the number of seeds that germinate?

3 What factors affect germination?

Task	Defining the problem	Choosing the method	Arriving at solutions
1	closed	closed	closed
2	closed	open	open
3	open	open	open

Build a better bridge

The bridge across the river sags when cars go across it.

If you were going to build a new bridge across the river which material would sag the most?

Ross and Kevin (age 11)
We placed the Nescafe tins 30 cm (1 ft) apart and put the plastic over the top making sure we didn't move the tin. Each tin was 12.5 cm high. We piled weights on top of the material until it sagged to 10 cm in height.

Material	Length between two tins	Amount of weight the material stood	Height we allowed it to sag to
Plastic	30 cm	800 g	10 cm
Wood	30 cm	1900 g	10 cm
Cardboard	30 cm	400 g	10 cm

The wood is the strongest material that we used and is therefore the most reliable for standing on between 2 objects.

Simon and Gavin
Method
We took 2 tripods and placed 4 different materials across them. We then put 50 g and 100 g weights in the middle. When the materials bent, we measured how far down it dipped.

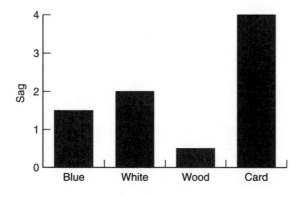

We found that the softer the material the farther it bent down.

The Assessment of Practical Work in Science (APWIS)

In Chapter 2, we saw how APWIS (Gott *et al.*, 1988) classified practical work into different types, but what is relevant here is that the authors also developed the definition of investigations further by using a classification of the variables within the investigation. The classification aimed to describe and then to assess the way in which pupils interpreted the nature of a variable.

APWIS used the terms 'categoric', 'discrete' and 'continuous'. A variable which is *categoric* is defined descriptively. For example, the type of insulation such as polystyrene or fibreglass is a categoric variable. A variable which is defined numerically but which takes only integer values is defined as a *discrete* variable. An example would be the number of layers of insulation around a heating tank. Finally, a *continuous* variable is one which is defined numerically and which can take any value, such as the thickness of an insulating layer of polystyrene beads.

Later, Foulds and Gott (1988), while acknowledging the influence of concepts and context (among other factors), developed a typology of tasks based largely on the variable structure of the investigation. They used the typology to suggest levels of difficulty associated with procedural understanding. They proposed grouping investigations into four main types, each with a different variable structure (Table 3.4).

From classroom experience, it was suggested that a type 1 question is likely to be easier for most pupils than a type 2 question. Many pupils opt to define a continuous variable as categoric: temperature may be defined in the categories hot, warm and cold. Type 3 is likely to be more difficult than either types 1 or 2, since it involves multivariate designs which many pupils find difficult. A variation of the multivariate design is the biological-type control experiment, where one value of the independent variable forms the control or standard. For example, if the investigation is to compare the effect of different fertilisers on growth, then one plant would be given none. Type 4 is more to do with technological problem-solving.

Investigative work in science

The project which gave rise to this book set out to research pupils' performance on all aspects of Science 1 (Sc1) in the National Curriculum, with particular reference to progression in children's understanding. We shall refer to this research as the 'NCC project' (Foulds *et al.*, 1992), since it was prepared for the National Curriculum Council (NCC), the research being jointly funded by the NCC and the DES.

The project was carried out between April 1990 and September 1991, with the specific aims of (a) documenting how Sc1 was being implemented, (b) identifying teaching methods which promote the effective integration of Sc1 with knowledge and understanding, and (c) identifying elements of progression in the levels of Sc1. The sample consisted of over 3500 children undertaking investigations covering Key Stages 1, 2 and 3. Of these, over 2000

Table 3.4 A typology of investigations (Foulds and Gott, 1988)

Question	Example
1 A single categoric variable	Which is the best type of insulation for a hot water tank?
2 A single continuous variable	Find out how the rate at which the water cools is dependent on the amount of water in the tank.
3 More than one independent variable	Is it the type of insulation material or its thickness which is keeping the water hot?
4 Constructional activities	Make the best insulated hot water tank

Table 3.5 Types of investigation used in the NCC project and their variable structure

Type	Independent variable 1	Independent variable 2	Dependent variable	Example
1	categoric	—	continuous	Find out which fruit gives the biggest voltage
2	continuous	—	continuous	Find out how the voltage depends on the distance between the strips of metal
3	categoric	categoric	continuous	Find out whether the voltage of the cell depends on the type of metal, the type of fruit or both of these things
4	continuous	continuous	continuous	Find out how the voltage of the cell depends on the distance between the metal strips and the amount of metal strip under the surface

children were in secondary education, these schools being in five education authorities in the north-east. Two hundred and ninety primary and secondary teachers from sixteen LEAs completed questionnaires regarding teachers' perceptions of Sc1. Fifty of these teachers were subsequently interviewed for validation purposes.

The NCC project defined investigations, following the APU line, as 'tasks which revolve around a practical problem for which there is a minimum of instructions'. The investigations in the project were selected on the basis of being accessible to the majority of pupils. Procedural complexity was manipulated through the variable structure of the task. Tasks were classified into four types according to the nature of the independent variable(s). The structures of these task types, with an example of each, are given in Table 3.5.

It will be seen that the NCC types 1 and 2 are the same as the APWIS types 1 and 2, but the multivariate designs are now divided into types 3 and 4. Discrete variables were not included. For clarity, the examples in Table 3.5 are drawn from one context, which is that of a 'fruit battery' where two different metals inserted into a fruit produce a voltage. The voltage depends on the area and type of the metals, the distance they are apart and the type of fruit. This example also serves to demonstrate

how a single context can be structured in a variety of ways to provide the basis for a range of complexity of investigations. These types of investigations will be referred to frequently in discussing the data arising from the project in the next two chapters.

A note on the limitations of focusing on the variable structure of investigations

If we take a restricted view of investigations as being solely to do with variables and numerical data, then large swathes of science, particularly chemistry and those elements of science bordering on technology, can become neglected. This has proved a problem with the National Curriculum in the UK. A broader viewpoint would consider not simply variable-based tasks, but also other types of investigative work summarised in Table 3.6.

Recalling our arguments of the last chapter, we can see that all of these types have in common the requirement, to a greater or lesser extent, that pupils *synthesise* skills and concepts of evidence in arriving at their solution. An example of a logical reasoning task will help to illustrate this point: in the context of a forensic-type detective activity with indicators or other qualitative tests, pupils are required to carry out

Table 3.6 Types of investigative work

Type of investigative work	Example
Variable-based	Type 1 (involving a *categoric* independent variable (see table 3.5) Type 2 (involving a *continuous* independent variable) Type 3 (involving more than one *categoric* independent variable) Type 4 (involving more than one *continuous* independent variable)
Logical reasoning tasks	Tasks involving the carrying out of a sequence of (often qualitative) tasks, the data from each of which structures subsequent tasks leading to a solution of the problem (forensic science, electrical fault-finding)
Measurement-focused	Often in science, engineering and technology the key problem is finding a way to measure a variable quantity which cannot be measured directly with available instrumentation
Constructional/engineering tasks	'Engineering' tasks aim to produce a solution to a problem and then test its effectiveness, rather than investigate the underlying factors. Making the best-insulated hot water tank, for instance, requires that the design be optimised
Constructional/technological	This type of task would encompass such activities as the construction of an electrical circuit where the criterion of success is concerned with whether or not the circuit does the job required
Explorations	The most open of the types involving pupils in raising the question and defining the task prior to developing a method of solution which may involve any of the types above (and other resource-based, non-practical work)

a relatively simple task, the pH of some solution perhaps, which then forms the basis for the selection of another test. Hence there is a progressive narrowing down of options – for example, if the pH is 4 then it couldn't be x or y, but it could be p or q. To distinguish p and q, pupils would need to do a flame test and so on. This is akin to the 'Find the cause of...' tasks of the APU. Here the synthesis of skills and concepts of evidence such as repeatability, reliability and validity are necessary to reach a solution.

Summary

The projects described in this chapter have led us to formulate a definition of investigations and to clarify what types of problems constitute investigations, while acknowledging that we are only focusing on one type of investigative work (variable-based investigations). Most of the research that has been done in investigative work has been concerned with tasks which can be defined by the variable structure we have described, the variable-based types in Table 3.6. The reasons for this may be that such tasks are quantitative and are easier to define in terms of assessment criteria. There is also the fact that Piagetian theory has had an influence on science education for many years and Piaget's work includes experiments which are largely variable-based.

The omission of other kinds of investigative work was recognised, but within the constraints of the APU and for the purposes of APWIS and NCC, the number and structural complexity of investigations had of necessity to be limited. The notion of concepts of evidence which we developed in the last chapter was also derived from variable-based tasks. In reality, research into procedural understanding is in its infancy and we should regard focusing on variable-based tasks as being no more than a start.

References

Assessment of Performance Unit (1985). *Science in Schools: Ages 13 and 15*. Research Report No. 3. London, HMSO.

Assessment of Performance Unit (1987). *Assessing Investigation at ages 13 and 15*. Science Report for Teachers: 9. London, HMSO.

Assessment of Performance Unit (1989). *National Assessment: The APU Science Approach*. London, HMSO.

Foulds, K. and Gott, R. (1988). Structuring investigations in the science curriculum. *Physics Education*, 23: 347-51.

Foulds, K., Gott, R. and Feasey, R. (1992). *Investigative Work in Science*. Durham, University of Durham.

Garrett, R.M. (1986). Problem-solving in science education. *Studies in Science Education*, 13: 70-95.

Gott, R. and Murphy, P. (1987). *Assessing Investigations at Ages 13 and 15*. APU Science Report for Teachers No. 9. London, DES.

Gott, R., Welford, G. and Foulds, K. (1988). *The Assessment of Practical Work in Science*. Oxford, Blackwell.

Jones, A.T., Simon, S.A., Black, P.J., Fairbrother, R.W. and Watson, J.R. (1992). *Open Work in Science: Development of Investigations in Schools*. Hatfield, Association for Science Education.

Simon, S.A. and Jones, A.T. (1992). *Open Work in Science: A Review of Existing Practice*. London, King's College London.

Watts, D.M. and Gilbert, J.K. (1989). The 'new learning': Research, development and the reform of school science education. *Studies in Science Education*, 16: 75-121.

CHAPTER 4

Pupils' performance of investigations in secondary schools: An overview

In the preceding chapter, we considered what kinds of practical work can be classified as investigations and, within that definition, how investigations might be further categorised into different types according to their structure.

In this chapter, we shall consider the main factors that are likely to influence overall performance. Chapter 5, will then take a detailed look at how children perform investigations and how they deploy their procedural understanding. This will enable us to find out which parts of an investigation most children do reasonably well and at which points they experience difficulty. Clearly, both aspects of research on children's performance have implications for teaching, progression and the issue of assessment, which we shall consider in subsequent chapters.

Factors affecting performance

What makes one investigation more difficult than another at a more general level? In this chapter, we shall try to answer this complex question with reference to existing research findings. Some of the possible factors that may influence the performance of children doing investigations are shown in Fig. 4.1

The APU research pointed to three of these key factors which influence the level of difficulty in any investigation:

- the difficulty of the substantive concepts involved (1 in Fig. 4.1);
- the context within which the investigation is set (4);
- the procedural complexity of the investigation (2), in terms of its variable structure.

The NCC project was designed to explore these same factors, together with two others: the 'openness' of the question and the age of the pupils. The research started from the hypothesis that, of these five factors, the major factors influencing performance would be:

- the substantive concepts which underpinned the task and the level of difficulty of the concepts within that subject area (1 in Fig. 4.1);
- the procedural complexity as defined by the task types 1–4 defined in Table 3.5 in the last chapter (2);
- the age of the pupils (3).

The secondary factors considered were:

- context (4); and
- openness (5).

The brief for the project was to investigate the relative effect, in so far as that is possible, of these various factors with a view to outlining the major

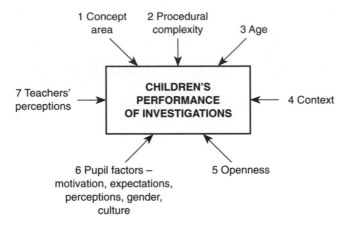

Fig. 4.1 Factors affecting pupils' performance of investigations

factors to be considered when building progression into the design of a curriculum and its assessment. The brief predetermines the research design to the extent that large samples are necessary, both of pupils and tasks, if any sort of generalisable statement is to be made. Before considering the research evidence about procedural understanding, we shall need to outline the sample and methodology of the NCC project in broad terms, to give the reader some idea of the weight which can be placed on the evidence.

The NCC sample, design, methodology and analysis

Sample

The breakdown of the sample into the numbers of children performing each type of investigation is shown in Table 4.1. In all, twenty-three different investigations were used. The data which were collected for type 4 investigations are restricted to two concept areas only and a smaller sample; generalisations should therefore be treated with particular caution.

Table 4.1 Sample size by age for each type of investigation

Type of investigation[a]	Number of investigations of each type	Sample size			
		Year 7 (age 11 years)	Year 8 (age 12 years)	Year 9 (age 13 years)	Total
1	10	271	395	256	922
2	7	158	410	69	637
3	4	76	298	101	475
4	2	84	47	43	174
Total	23	589	1150	469	2208

[a] See Table 3.5 for definition.

The design

The investigations were chosen to give details on the influence of the predicted major and secondary factors on performance as well as the interaction of some of these factors, as will be shown below.

Conceptual demand or difficulty

The investigations were chosen so that they covered a range of substantive concepts (see Table 4.2). Some groups of investigations were designed to test the effect of increasing conceptual difficulty within one concept area. An example of a group of investigations which all concern forces and motion is given in Table 4.3.

Procedural complexity

Procedural complexity was defined by the variable structure of the task (for definitions of types of investigations, see Table 3.5). To recap briefly here, types 1 and 2 involve a single independent variable, while types 3 and 4 both have two independent variables. Types 1 and 3 involve categoric independent variables, while types 2 and 4 involve continuous independent variables. The tasks in the concept area of forces and motion are outlined in Table 4.4.

The interaction of concepts and procedural complexity

This interaction was tested by designing investigations in a range of concept areas spread across

Table 4.2 Concept areas of the NCC investigations

Concept area	Context and concepts underlying the tasks
Electricity from chemical reactions	A fruit battery, in which pupils are asked to investigate the effects of factors such as separation of the electrodes, their depth and the types of fruit on voltage (see Table 3.5)
Forces – the flexibility of materials	Bridges (the effects of factors such as type of material, width or length of material, or the weight on the bridge on the amount the 'bridge' sags)
Dissolving	Sugar (or a 'chemical') dissolving in tea or coffee (the effects of factors such as the type of sugar or the temperature of the water on the dissolving time)
Forces and motion	A model car fired from an elastic band launcher (the effects of factors such as the amount of energy in the elastic band or how much it is stretched, on the distance travelled or the speed)
Heat transfer	Keeping drinks warm (the effect of the material of a cup on the rate of heat loss)
Energy transfer	Fuels (find out which is the best fuel)

Table 4.3 An example of varying the concept difficulty in a forces and motion investigation (type 2 tasks)

The concept(s) underlying the variables	Investigation
Distance only	Find out how the amount of stretch (of an elastic band) affects the distance travelled (by a model car – in practice, a margarine tub)
Speed and length	Find out how the speed of your model depends on how much you stretch the elastic band
Speed and energy	Find out how the speed of your model depends on the amount of energy stored in the elastic band

Table 4.4 An example of varying procedural complexity within one concept area

FORCES – the flexibility of materials	
Type 1	Find out whether the amount by which the bridge sags depends on the type of material used
Type 2	Find out how the length of the bridge affects how much it sags
Type 3	Find out whether the amount by which the bridge sags depends on: • the type of the material, or • the width of the material, or • both of these things
Type 4	Find out how the sag of the bridge depends on: • the weight of the person, and • the length of the plank

Table 4.5 Varying the procedural complexity across different concept areas

Procedural complexity	Concept area					
	Electricity from chemical reactions	*Forces – the flexibility of materials*	*Dissolving*	*Forces and motion*	*Heat transfer*	*Energy transfer*
Type 1	√	√	√		√	√
Type 2	√	√	√	√		
Type 3	√	√	√	√		
Type 4	√	√				

the four different types of investigations. Table 4.5 shows how the investigations were spread across type and concept area.

Age

The design of the sample (Table 4.1) covered pupils in years 7, 8 and 9 (ages 11–13). The total sample of some 2200 pupils comprised some 700 groups. Although investigations were carried out by groups, individuals within these groups were asked to write up their investigation independently.

Context

Three pairs of investigations in the concept areas of dissolving and heat transfer were varied in that one of the pair was set in an 'everyday' context and the other in a 'scientific' context. Some examples are shown in Table 4.6.

Table 4.6 Varying the context (types 1 and 2 only)

Scientific	'Everyday'
Find out which chemical dissolves fastest. (type 1)	Find out which type of sugar dissolves fastest.
Find out how the temperature of the water affects how quickly sodium hydrogen carbonate dissolves. (type 2)	How does the temperature of the water affect how quickly the sugar dissolves?

Openness

Finally, two pairs of investigations were varied in the degree of 'openness' (Table 4.7). Openness here refers to the way in which the task is presented.

Table 4.7 The openness of tasks (type 1 only)

(More) open	(More) closed
Which fuel is best?	Which fuel gives out the most heat?
Which cup is best?	Which cup would keep a drink hot longest?

Methodology

Each school taking part in the NCC research was asked to carry out the investigations during normal science lessons. Following a half-day training session, teachers were asked to complete parts of an observation checklist while the pupils were carrying out the investigations, some elements of which are given in Table 4.8.

Basic equipment for each task was provided centrally but schools were asked to provide other equipment, if requested by the pupils. The final data consisted of pupils' individual accounts of their investigation together with an observation checklist for each group completed by the class teacher.

The analysis

The pupils' scripts were compared with the teachers' checklists and any suspect data in terms of internal consistency discarded (approximately 5 per cent). Scores which were derived from the teachers' checklist data were validated by the researcher against pupil scripts which had been analysed independently. Additional data derived from pupil scripts were added to the computer data set.

The data were analysed using a 'task score', which is a summative score based on all the individual elements of the investigation reflecting the pupils' overall performance. It was calculated by simply adding up the ticks in the boxes on the checklist. For the purposes of the analysis, the task score was broken down into three parts: the variable score, the data score and the interpretation score. The variable score was based on the checkpoints relating to the identification of the variables in the task. The data score also consisted of several checkpoints relating to measurement and representation of the data, while the interpretation score (a 0–1 score) was based on an overview of the whole

Table 4.8 Examples of items in the teacher's observation checklist

Variable types	√ or ×	Comment
Independent variable 1 defined as categoric		
Independent variable 1 defined as continuous		
Dependent variable defined as categoric		
Dependent variable defined as continuous		
Putting variables into practice		
Independent variable put into practice effectively		
Appropriate variables controlled		
Measurement		
Scale adequate		
Accuracy appropriate		
Recording of results		
Data handling		
Data recorded in table		
Data recorded in bar chart		
Data recorded in line graph		

task and reflected whether or not the pupil was able to make an appropriate interpretation and generalisation from his or her data.

During the analysis, it became clear that the overall task score behaved in a very similar way to two of the part scores, the variable and data scores, but frequently quite differently to the interpretation score. The results that are presented here, therefore, will only refer to the task and interpretation scores. For a more detailed discussion, the reader is referred to the original research report (Foulds *et al.*, 1992). Suffice it to say here that the scores were analysed using analysis of variance and that differences are significant at the 0.001 level unless otherwise stated.

The resulting data will be used extensively in this and the following chapter, together with data from other research findings. We shall continue by considering the findings concerning each of the factors in Fig. 4.1 in turn.

The effect of substantive concepts

What effects do substantive concepts have on performance? Both the APU and the NCC projects suggest, not surprisingly perhaps, that substantive concepts strongly affect performance. The APU team distinguishes between 'everyday' concepts (that is, commonly known concepts) and 'taught science concepts'. Although the investigations used in their research were those requiring little in the way of taught science concepts, they still noted their strong influence:

> The results have shown that it is hazardous to attempt to generalise about children's performance in the various investigations. The particular subject matter of a problem has a very strong influence on performance, introducing a number of variables whose influence cannot easily be disentangled. This is borne out both by the detailed accounts of performance in an investigation as a whole,...and the analysis of results in terms of various component parts of the investigations.
>
> (Russell *et al.*, 1988.)

In the NCC project, the data were analysed to examine the effect of concept area alone by averaging performance across all tasks within each of the four principal concept areas in which the majority of the data were collected. Figure 4.2 shows how performance, in terms of the task and interpretation scores, varied between the four concept areas.

Both the task and interpretation scores revealed significant differences in performance between the different concept areas, suggesting that the underlying concept has a strong influence on performance. Of these four concept areas, one would expect electricity to be the most difficult but neither of the scores showed this to be true. However, if we look more closely at the investigations themselves, we can distinguish between the concepts that are embedded in the investigation and the concepts which are actually essential to performing a particular investigation successfully. For example, the investigations concerning electricity (which are described in Table 3.5) do not necessitate the critical application of any concept

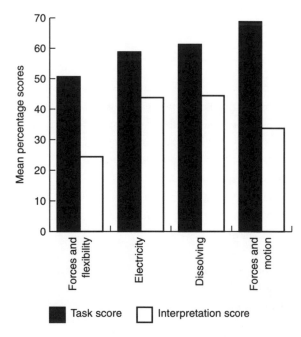

Fig. 4.2 Task and interpretation scores for four concept areas

of electricity for successful performance. Children in the sample interpreted their results adequately without reference to the underlying concept. If an explanation had been required, then it is likely that the children would have found it more difficult. Looking at the interpretation score, both tasks involving forces proved to be more difficult to interpret than the other two concept areas (electricity and dissolving). We suggest a reason for the differences between the two forces and motion tasks in the next chapter. What we might mention here is that, rather than the concepts themselves, it is the associated context – the apparatus and its familiarity perhaps – which is the more significant factor.

The effect of the level of difficulty of the concept

The example in Table 4.9 shows that as the difficulty within a concept area increases, in this case from 'distance' to 'speed and energy', so the task score decreases slightly. In contrast, the interpretation score rose slightly, from a low value of some 30 per cent.

This seems to make no sense at all. Energy and speed are clearly more difficult ideas than simply measuring how far the car travelled. So why should there be so little difference, a difference which barely reaches statistical significance? What the data point to is that the effects of concepts on performance are by no means as straightforward as perhaps might be imagined. One part of the explanation may lie in the constraints of the task itself. Given the apparatus available, there are very few alternative sets of variables to measure,

Table 4.9 Task scores for increasing conceptual difficulty in the forces and motion investigations

The concept(s) underlying the variables	Task score (%)
Distance	68
Speed and length	66
Speed and energy	62

although there are different ways of proceeding from there on. Pupils then, presumably, identify that the distance the elastic band launcher is pulled back will be related to energy, no matter how tenuous their grip on the concept of energy might be. A similar argument applies to speed with the exception that very few pupils indeed actually calculated a speed, usually being content with the component parts of distance and time.

The effect of procedural complexity

The APU found that where an investigation involves one independent and one dependent variable, most pupils were able to design the investigation successfully. However, when two independent variables are involved, as in the woodlice investigation (Table 3.2) where dampness and light are the independent variables, the percentage of pupils able to handle the interaction fell markedly, in this particular case to 43 per cent (Archenhold et al., 1988). Of these pupils, 21 per cent manipulated all four environments together, while 22 per cent set up one combination at a time. In some cases, four separate little environments were created, separated by a considerable distance equivalent to many 'woodlice lengths'. A number of woodlice would then be placed in the middle of the four environments and expected to decide from afar, without being allowed time to wander from one to the other, where they would like to go. When the four environments were tested one at a time, the pupils were forced to rely on some independent measure of woodlice contentment – for example, one pupil decided that happiness in woodlice was indicated when 'they lay on their backs and wriggled'.

In this case, the problem of two independent variables was compounded by problems of deciding how to measure 'happiness' as well as notions of animal variation. In the swingboard investigation (Gott and Murphy, 1987) where there was no such complication, of the pupils who were asked to investigate the effect of length *and* width on the rate of the swing, 44 per cent still failed to test adequately both independent variables.

We saw in the last chapter how the NCC project divided procedural complexity into four types of investigations (see Table 3.5) in terms of the number and type of independent variables involved. When the data are analysed by investigation type disregarding age, concept area and context, the pattern that emerges is different for the task scores and interpretation scores (Fig. 4.3).

If we consider the task scores first, there are two underlying trends. First, there is the failure of some pupils to identify independent variables as continuous, which makes type 2 and type 4 investigations appear to be more difficult than types 1 and 3. Superimposed on this pattern is a gradual deterioration in performance, as measured by the task score, with task type. This deterioration can be attributed to a more general factor, the overall complexity of the task, represented by the numbers of independent variables involved.

Turning to the interpretation score, the pattern here shows a gradual decline in percentage score with task type. The difference in the behaviour of these two scores can be explained by considering what the two scores represent. The task score is a summation of a disparate set of actions. If a pupil makes an error of task definition, for instance, then this will reduce his or her overall score somewhat. But since the majority of the individual elements are to do with the carrying out of the investigation and recording the data, which still apply even if the task has been wrongly defined, then the fall in the overall score is small. The task score, then, represents the ability of pupils to perform *elements* of the task successfully. The interpretation score, on the other hand, relies more on the ability to *synthesise* the key elements of the task and to present findings which relate to the original task as set, rather than as subsequently defined by the pupil. We will return to this issue in the context of assessment in a later chapter.

The effect of age

At the time of the APU survey, overall pupil performance on investigations between ages 13 and 15 was not noticeably different. Among the differences that were observed was a greater tendency among 13-year-olds to control *all* possible control variables whether or not they were relevant. More 15-year-olds used tables to record their data and they also tended to revise the design of their investigation more often than the younger pupils. In the 'survival' investigation (Which fabric would keep you warmer?), more 15-year-olds (56 per cent) than 13-year-olds (44 per cent) measured both the initial and the final temperatures, but this sort of improvement was attributed to increased conceptual understanding rather than investigatory skill (Archenhold *et al.*, 1988). In the longitudinal study, where the same pupils were tested at ages 12 and 14, there was evidence of progression (Strang *et al.*, 1991), although only two investigations were observed.

The NCC project also found that there was progression in the performance of investigations with age (years 7, 8 and 9) in terms of both the task and interpretation scores (Fig. 4.4). The changes in the overall task score were relatively small, certainly less than the effect of different concept areas. The change in the ability to interpret and generalise from the data was more marked, however.

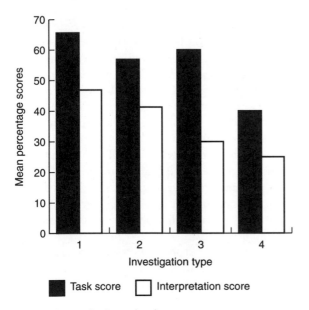

Fig. 4.3 Scores by investigation type

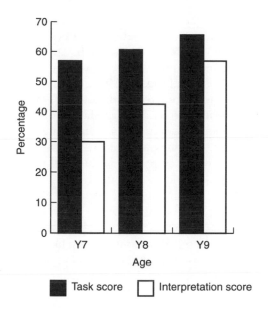

Fig. 4.4 Task and interpretation scores by age

The effect of context

Gott and Murphy (1987), in considering the effect of the everyday context of most of their investigations, wrote: 'The evidence so far suggests that the problem context does influence pupils' performance but that the effect is not a simple one.' They noted that a scientific context can inhibit some pupils' performance and that this effect seems to be linked to specific concept areas. For example, if a pupil perceives electricity as a difficult topic, then he or she may transfer this perception to any investigation set in this context, which in turn can affect performance. On the other hand, the APU found that an everyday context can lead some pupils to the idea that an everyday answer is all that is required and the notion that 'we should only behave scientifically when the task looks scientific'.

On two investigations, one set in an everyday and one in a scientific context, pupils were more systematic and quantitative when performing the investigation set in a scientific context. Strang *et al.* (1991), in reporting the work of the APU, suggested that the scientific context 'cues pupils

into working in a scientific way by reminding them of investigations they have done previously... The importance of the context here is in providing a frame of reference for pupils which allows them to access previous experience.'

The NCC project used three investigations which were presented in both everyday and scientific contexts. The performance of the children in terms of the task scores and interpretation scores and disregarding other factors are shown in Table 4.10. Both scores show that performance was better when the context was scientific as opposed to everyday. It may be that if children are asked to find out about types of 'chemicals' rather than sugar in an everyday setting, it focuses them in the direction of solubility and of 'being scientific'. The everyday setting almost seems to distract them from the science of the task and leads them to think that non-scientific answers will suffice. Perhaps the most significant message here is that children do not see that it is necessary to 'be scientific' in everyday situations.

It is also important to remember that the influence of both the concept area and the context is linked to the gender and culture of the pupils. Johnson and Murphy (1986), in discussing the findings of the APU, pointed to the gender differences in the type of experiences pupils have outside school. We cannot assume that particular concepts or contexts are familiar to all pupils.

The effect of openness

The APU tasks did not include open questions such as those used in the NCC project. In the latter, two pairs of investigations were varied in the degree of openness (see Table 4.11). The effect of openness was not significantly different in terms

Table 4.10 Everyday vs scientific contexts

	Everyday	Scientific
Task score	58	66
Interpretation score	46	62

Table 4.11 Open versus closed tasks. Note that the differences between task scores are *not* significant

	More open	*More closed*
Task score	62	65
Interpretation score	44	79

of the task score from that for the more directed, closed tasks. It is encouraging to note that *all* of the children who were presented with an open task chose appropriate variables in defining the task. Another facet of the more open tasks was that a number of children attempted multiple tests on several different dependent variables, in an attempt to form some overview of suitable properties. This approach may be modelled on reality since, for example, the consumer would want to know about more than one property to decide which was the 'best' fuel.

However, Table 4.11 shows that the interpretation scores of the open and closed tasks were significantly different. Pupils were better at interpreting the data and producing an appropriate generalisation (which as we have argued earlier, represents their ability to synthesise various elements) in closed tasks than in open ones. In open tasks, they tended to regress to qualitative comparisons, as indeed they did in the case of everyday versus scientific contexts.

The relative significance of these factors

The important issue here is not that concepts, context or task complexity influence performance – of course they do. The issue in planning curricula and, particularly, assessment, is how great are these effects one relative to another? Examining the data in the barcharts in some detail, we can suggest tentatively that procedural complexity and the concept area have a major effect on both the task and interpretation scores. But openness and age also have a significant influence on the interpretation score.

We have argued that the interpretation score better represents the ability to synthesise all the elements of the task. As the complexity of the task increases (whether it is due to more or more complex variables, or more difficult or unfamiliar concepts and contexts, or having to grapple with defining a more open task), so does the ability needed to hold it all together. These factors do not affect the task score so much because, even if a pupil has lost the thread, he or she can still go on and do something, even if that something has lost its direction. The message for teaching is that we must place greater emphasis on this ability to keep the whole task in view.

The data further suggest that relatively closed type 1 tasks, set in concept areas where the ideas revolve around familiar ideas such as length and, furthermore, in scientific contexts, are likely to be a good starting point for curriculum planning. From there on, progression in the type of tasks presented to pupils will need to be tightly monitored to ensure that too many factors are not changed too quickly, so halting pupils' development.

If we analyse the same data using multiple linear regression, then we find that concept area, age and procedural complexity explain only about 10 per cent of the variation. Other factors such as motivation or pupil expectations will have a major influence. On the other hand, given that the pupils or schools were not matched in any way and that investigations are a very complex activity, it is not surprising that there is a lot of 'noise' (or random effects that mask trends) in the data. But it is still true that the effect of the underlying concept is a very significant one, on both scores, and this finding has considerable implications when making decisions about the concept demands of tasks intended for the assessment of procedural understanding and the number of different concept areas that must be covered, if we are to get a reliable and valid 'handle' on pupil ability.

Motivation, expectations and perceptions

The first and most important point to note is that pupils do remarkably well in investigations. They very rarely fail to carry out the task in some way. It is this very success, we suggest, that is responsible for the high motivation among pupils doing investigations, that was reported by many schools engaged in the NCC research. Watts (1991) has also commented on the sense of empowerment and ownership that this kind of problem-solving generates.

In 1981, the APU team (Harlen *et al.*, 1981) asked their assessors to rate the motivation of 11-year-old pupils as they undertook investigations. The results across six investigations are shown in Table 4.12. Apparently, even under assessment conditions and at a time when most pupils had had no experience of investigative work, almost half the pupils found investigations to be both interesting and enjoyable. When an assessor was asked whether pupils cooperated and were interested in the investigations, the reply was: 'Without exception. Once embarked upon tasks they became really involved and most were determined to solve the problem no matter how long it took' (Archenhold *et al.*, 1988). The degree to which pupils feel in control of their own learning is a significant factor here, but one in which there has been little research, particularly in practical science.

Simon and Jones (1992) discuss several factors that can affect pupil motivation and so influence performance. These factors include 'learning expectations', that is, what the pupil expects to learn in a science practical. For instance, if the emphasis in previous practicals has always been on facts and concepts, pupils may miss the point of a practical which is designed to improve procedural understanding and may even consider it to be a pointless exercise and therefore not perform well. 'Expectation of completion of the task' refers to what the pupil thinks the teacher wants. For instance, he or she may associate satisfactory completion of the task with being busy 'doing' or writing copiously rather than reflecting and thinking about the nature and purpose of the task. Performance may also be affected if pupils believe that they know 'the right answer' and see this as a way of obtaining good marks. They may then write a convincing report based on previous ideas ignoring their own data, whether or not the data agree with their prediction of what the right answer should be and regardless of the teacher's guidance. Again we have recently seen evidence in the UK that some pupils are purposely gearing their work to achieve particular assessment goals.

A pupil's perception of his or her own ability to learn in science practicals is also likely to influence performance. If he or she has experienced failure in the past, then subsequent practicals are likely to be approached negatively, expecting to fail again. Such children will avoid any challenge and tend to give up easily. This motivational style is known as 'learned helplessness'. At the other extreme are children who perceive difficult tasks as challenging rather than threatening.

Perhaps the most important point here, and one easily overlooked in the search for complex reasons for high motivation, is that we are all motivated by success. No matter what it is we are asked to do, if we succeed, and continue to do so especially when the going gets tough, then we tend to persist. If the opposite is the case, then confidence plummets. There is nothing motivating about being told that something you cannot do would be good for you if you *could* do it. Investigations, because of their very openness, allow all pupils to feel that they are successful to some degree, as indeed they are. So in the midst of our search for progression, let us not forget that making things too hard, too soon, is in no one's interest.

Finally, the peer interaction that occurs in group work influences performance. Collaborative skills can enhance learning, providing support for the less confident pupils. Occasionally, of course, group work can 'go wrong' and it is here that the role of the teacher is again crucial. While we recognise the importance of all these factors, in the main they are outside the control of the teacher.

Table 4.12 Motivation (Harlen *et al.*, 1981)

Category	Percentage of pupils
Evidence of real interest	47
Willing but no great enthusiasm	48
Uninterested	4

Teachers' perceptions

When we consider the factors that influence pupil performance in investigations, it seems sensible to assume that both the teacher and teaching have an effect. But does the way investigations are taught, which depends on the teacher's views as to what they are for, make any difference? Sharp and Green (1975) noted the significance of teachers' beliefs as to the role(s) that they adopt and how these beliefs influence their practice. For instance, a teacher who believes that investigations are about 'allowing children to discover things for themselves', may adopt an extreme non-interventionist role acting only as a manager and provider of resources. What do we know about teachers' views?

The research data are sparse in this regard. The NCC project included a questionnaire which was designed to probe teachers' understanding of AT1 in the general context of practical work in science. The questionnaire was completed by 290 teachers, 123 of whom taught at the secondary level, 85 at the junior level and 82 at the infant level. The teachers were also asked to submit sample material of the type they use for an investigation. A sample of 50 teachers was interviewed shortly after the questionnaire had been sent out and the resulting data used to validate the questionnaire.

Teachers were asked to order five possible aims for practical work (Table 4.13). The data showed that, at the infant teacher level, the emphasis was quite clearly on the idea of observation as the key

aim of science. Junior teachers see a move towards concept understanding, whether through illustration or enquiry, a move which is further emphasised at secondary level when observation has fallen very much lower down the list. However, when teachers were asked about the purpose of *investigative work*, the results showed a somewhat confused picture (Table 4.14). There was a general move towards 'processes and skills', that ubiquitous and ill-defined phrase that we came across in an earlier chapter.

The most telling information came from the samples of investigations that had been submitted. The samples were analysed by a process of grouping the material into categories with obvious characteristics in common. Only then was a descriptive title given to each of the groupings, the titles being based on the definitions we have adopted in this book. The major categories are shown in Table 4.15.

What we see now is that infant teachers, and to a lesser extent teachers of juniors, based much of their work on simple observation activities despite a claim for increased emphasis on 'processes and skills'. At secondary level, the samples were mainly 'guided investigations' or investigations with a 'recipe' provided. What is certain is that there was little obvious correlation between the professed aims and the samples. The interpretation of this questionnaire was problematic due to the difficulty of ensuring that all involved were using the terms in the same way. As a conse-

Table 4.13 Teachers' perceptions of the aims of practical work

Most important aim of practical work	Year 1 (%)	Year 3 (%)	Year 7 (%)
Concept illustration/consolidation	23	29	39
Raising questions and devising solutions	22	35	31
Observation	52	29	10
Concept discovery (enquiry)	1	6	9
Skills	1	0	11

Table 4.14 Teachers' perceptions of the purpose of investigative work

Major stated purpose of investigative work	Year 1 (%)	Year 3 (%)	Year 7 (%)
Skills or processes	19	29	29
Concept discovery (enquiry)	22	20	18
Use or refine concepts	9	12	18
Raise questions or test ideas	15	16	14
Enjoyment or motivation	10	11	7
Observation	3	2	1

Table 4.15 Types of activity used by teachers as 'investigations'

Type of activity	Year 1 (%)	Year 3 (%)	Year 7 (%)
Skills development (measuring, manipulating)	1	1	8
Design and build	11	11	8
Illustrative experiment	1	1	7
Guided 'investigation': teacher directed	3	12	19
Observation and recording	53	36	5
Investigation including: free access to apparatus, external reference, minimal instructions, choice of recording format	1	1	15

quence, it is probably only safe to say that the word 'investigation' was being used to describe a range of practical work. There seemed little in the way of a common philosophy as to how teachers perceived 'investigations'.

Evidence from HMI surveys

In the UK, there have been annual inspections of a sample of primary and secondary schools which have examined science in schools since the introduction of the National Curriculum in 1989. The UK National Curriculum is based on an assessment system defined by ten levels within four attainment targets (ATs). The attainment targets are centred loosely around investigations (Sc1), life and living processes (Sc2), materials and their properties (Sc3) and physical processes (Sc4). These four attainment targets are assessed individually. Each of the ten levels is in turn defined by more precise objectives or Statements of Attainment.

The first annual inspection during the school year 1989–90 found that: 'Too much of the Year 7 work either insufficiently linked Sc1 to the other Attainment Targets or was narrowly focused on individual Statements of Attainment' (HMI, 1991). The second report (during 1990–1)

found that in secondary schools investigative work was being blocked at a low level: 'In much of the work pupils were given insufficient opportunity to develop higher skills of hypothesising, designing investigations or interpreting evidence. Pupil achievement in AT1 was thus being blocked at level 4 in many schools' (HMI, 1992). The third and most recent report (during 1991–2) found the situation relatively unchanged in middle and secondary schools:

> Investigative work had increased and pupils were becoming more adept in planning and carrying out simple investigations. However their ability to tackle more complex investigations, to hypothesise, identify variables and evaluate the outcomes of investigations, remained weak. As a result, work above level 4 in Sc1 continued to be rare.
>
> For pupils of all abilities there was a lack of challenge and under-expectation in work related to Sc1.

(HMI, 1993)

It would seem, therefore, that there has been a gradual increase in the proportion of investigative work being carried out in secondary schools but that teaching of the more complex investigations is infrequent. It is also apparent that opportunities for pupils to focus on the nature of evidence in investigations are few. The impression from reading these reports is one of teachers engaging with individual skills and concepts of evidence, but not with their synthesis.

The above is consonant with the NCC findings that many teachers were confused as to the role and purpose of investigations. We should note, however, that the questionnaire was carried out shortly after the formal introduction of investigations into the curriculum in the UK. The HMI reports suggest that the situation may be improving.

A note on the effect of teaching about investigations and concepts of evidence

Of the schools which took part in the NCC research, a small number were actively working in the area of investigations, developing some of the teaching ideas and schemes of work which we put forward in Chapters 6 and 7. The remainder were not very far along the road at all. It is of interest, then, to compare how such schools fared. Because the investigations were spread out, with no school doing all of them, it is not possible to make a direct comparison based on any one investigation. What can be done, however, is to reduce the task scores (the overall pattern for interpretation scores being very similar) to 'z-scores'. This technique turns a percentage score on a particular task into one based on the mean for that task over all the groups which carried it out. It is now possible to compare one investigation with another, in relative terms if not absolutely.

So which schools did well? The school which was furthest ahead in its development of investigative work came out top of the list. Others similarly advanced, were all near the top. But what about the differences in the ability level of the schools' intake? It might be that the schools at the top of the list are the ones with the most able pupils anyway. To test this, the best that can be done with the data as they stand, is to refer back to league tables of GCSE results (which are examinations taken at the end of compulsory school). We can use these as some sort of, admittedly doubtful, measure of the overall ability level of a school's catchment.

If we aggregate investigation data for a school and compare it with its GCSE scores, the pattern in Fig. 4.5 emerges. Clearly, there is little, if any,

correlation between performance in investigations and this crude measure of ability. The school with the highest score on investigations is almost at the bottom of the league table of GCSEs, while the school at the top of the GCSE league is almost at the bottom of the investigation score. What this hints at, and it can be little more than a hint, is that performance on investigations does not rise and fall with overall attainment by educational osmosis. Rather, it suggests that investigative ideas *can* be taught and taught successfully. And, equally importantly from the point of view of motivation, pupils who are not likely to do very well at GCSE, are able to succeed in investigative work. Of course, it could be the Hawthorne effect operating – the school developing investigations may simply be more enthusiastic, which is transmitted to the pupils. We do not know. Only more careful research planned with that question in mind will tell us.

Summary

To recap, the research we have examined shows that:

- Of the factors tested in the NCC project, substantive concepts had the strongest influence on performance. We have discussed how this influence is sometimes unexpected.
- Progression within investigations which are based on variables is influenced by both the type and number of variables.
- Pupil performance improves with age. The ability to interpret and generalise improves more than the overall task performance which is relatively little affected.
- Pupils do less well in investigations set in 'everyday' contexts than in scientific contexts.
- Open contexts are more difficult than closed contexts.
- Motivation appears to be high, although the evidence to support this statement is of an anecdotal nature. Expectations and pupil perceptions may have a significant influence on

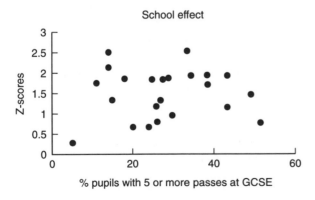

Fig. 4.5 Performance and GCSE passes for individual schools

performance, but there is a paucity of research in these areas.

- Teachers' views of investigations at the time of the NCC study appear to have been both diverse and confused. Although there has been a gradual increase in the proportion of investigative work in schools, it tends to be at the lower levels. Older pupils are not being allowed the opportunity to tackle the more complex investigations and their associated concepts of evidence.
- The effect of focusing teaching on concepts of evidence is that pupils' performance improves. The data also suggest that children who perform well generally in their GCSE examinations do not necessarily perform well in investigations and vice versa.

References

Archenhold, F., Bell, J., Donnelly, J., Johnson, S. and Welford, G. (1988). *Science at Age 15: A Review of APU Survey Findings, 1980–84*. London, HMSO.

Foulds, K., Gott, R. and Feasey, R. (1992). 'Investigative work in science'. Unpublished research report, University of Durham.

Gott, R. and Murphy, P. (1987). *Assessing Investigations at Ages 13 and 15*. APU Science Report for Teachers No. 9. London, HMSO.

Harlen, W., Black, P. and Johnson, S. (1981). *Science in Schools: Age 11*. APU Science Report for Teachers No.1. London, HMSO.

Her Majesty's Inspectorate (1991). *Science Key Stages 1, 2 and 3: A Report by HMI on the First Year, 1989–90*. London, HMSO.

Her Majesty's Inspectorate (1992). *Science Key Stages 1, 2 and 3: A Report by HMI on the Second Year, 1990–91*. London, HMSO.

Her Majesty's Inspectorate (1993). *Science Key Stages 1, 2 and 3: A Report by HMI on the Third Year, 1991–2*. London, HMSO.

Johnson, S. and Murphy, P. (1986). *Girls and Physics: Reflections on APU Survey Findings*. APU Occasional Paper No. 4. London, HMSO.

Russell, T., Black, P., Harlen, W., Johnson, S. and Palacio, D. (1988). *Science at Age 11: A Review of APU Survey Findings, 1980–84*. London, HMSO.

Sharp, R. and Green, A. (1975). *Education and Social Control: A Study in Progressive Primary Education*. London, Routledge and Kegan Paul.

Simon, S.A. and Jones, A.T. (1992). *Open Work in Science: A Review of Existing Practice*. London, King's College London.

Strang, J., Daniels, S. and Bell, J. (1991). *Planning and Carrying Out Investigations*. Assessment Matters No. 6. London, SEAC/EMU.

Watts, M. (1991). *The Science of Problem-solving: A Practical Guide for Teachers*. London, Heinemann/Cassell Educational.

CHAPTER 5

The performance of investigations in secondary schools: A detailed look

In this chapter, we shall take a detailed look at how procedural and conceptual understanding influence children's performance as they carry out an investigation. We shall start by considering the skills that children need in order to do investigations. Then we shall identify the concepts of evidence that children find difficult and the extent to which the substantive concepts of science influence performance at various stages. This kind of diagnostic information will allow teachers to focus their teaching on specific points of difficulty.

Skills

We discussed earlier how basic skills can be seen to underpin procedural understanding (see Fig. 2.1). It is clear that children should have the skills necessary to carry out investigations, otherwise poor performance can simply be a reflection of the lack of a particular skill (or skills). What does the research tell us about children's basic skills?

The APU looked at pupils' skills of measurement and in a small progression study carried out between 1987 and 1989 (Archenhold *et al.*, 1991) found, not unexpectedly, that there were noticeable trends in making and using measurements with age. Children were asked to:

- read pre-set instruments;
- use measuring instruments; and
- estimate measurements.

The APU found that children improved with age from making qualitative to quantitative measurements, from using non-standard measures to using standard measuring instruments and from using simple to more complex instruments. Most progress was made in *reading* instruments rather than *using* them or *estimating* measurements. Overall, the study found that reading instruments was heavily dependent on the nature of the instrument being used, although children often made mistakes with minor divisions in instrument scales regardless of the instrument.

An example will serve to illustrate this point. In the APU survey (Welford *et al.*, 1985), pupils were asked to read voltmeters and ammeters which had been set up in a 'circus' practical. The reading of the scales presented very considerable problems, problems that are probably independent of the quantity that is being measured. For the voltmeter, the scale was in single whole numbers with divisions of 0.1 on a range of 0 to 5 V. The scale of the ammeter read from 0 to 1 A with major divisions of 0.2 A and minor divisions of 0.02 A. Not unexpectedly, reading the voltmeter was found to be much easier: 61 per cent of 15-year-olds read the scale on the voltmeter accurately, whereas only 11 per cent did so for the ammeter. The emphasis in a task such as this is on the skills (as we have defined them in Chapter 2) of reading the instruments. But in this particular case, the key factor is the understanding – or lack of it – of decimals in maths.

Lack of understanding concerning the substantive concepts of current and voltage was highlighted in another APU task where pupils were given a circuit which was already connected and asked to insert an ammeter and then a voltmeter to measure current and voltage, respectively. Only 9 per cent of 15-year-old pupils connected both instruments correctly. Thirty-nine per cent chose the voltmeter for measuring current and 17 per cent chose the ammeter to measure voltage. Written questions also revealed that, 'for the majority of pupils the units for current could almost have been a random selection from "volts" or "amps"' (Gott, 1984). In this case, the 'skill' *was* demonstrated; they did connect the meters. But the understanding needed to know 'which to connect where' was missing.

The APU progression study also considered graphing skills by means of written tests (Figs 5.1. and 5.2). They found that the majority of pupils, by the age of 14, had grasped the basic skills needed to construct a line graph, although less than half were able to draw a line of best fit. These findings suggest that pupils had grasped the skill of graph construction but not the underlying concept of patterns.

Only 20 per cent of 12-year-olds and 71 per cent of 14-year-olds actually connected the points of the graph at all despite having plotted them accurately,

and of those who did, the majority did so using straight lines. Archenhold *et al.* (1991) conclude that: 'It would appear that, despite some progression in drawing a line of best fit, a considerable proportion of pupils at both ages did not appreciate the continuity of line graphs.' There was also some confusion between bar charts or 'stick graphs' and line graphs, with many children drawing bar charts or 'stick graphs' when they had been asked to draw a line graph. Archenhold *et al.* (1991) write: 'for many pupils at age 12, the required curricular progress from "bar chart" to "line graph" construction is likely to be a *substantial* "step forward"'.

We see, then, that the basic skills needed to construct graphs are not such a major problem, although there are indications here that while children can recall the skill of constructing a graph they may not understand its purpose. We must note, however, that we are considering isolated written tests. We shall see in the next section how children use graphs in whole investigations.

The overall pattern emerging is that, in secondary schools, it is either substantive concepts in maths or science, or concepts of evidence underlying the skills that are the major problem, rather than the mechanical aspects of investigative work.

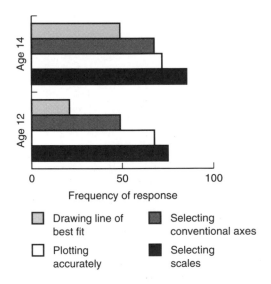

Fig. 5.1 Development of graph construction skills

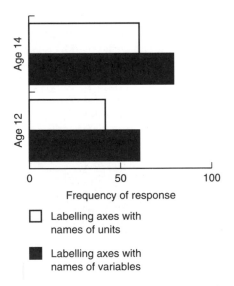

Fig. 5.2 Development of graph communication skills

Concepts of evidence

What does research tell us about how children understand the concepts of evidence as defined in Chapter 2, which lie at the heart of procedural understanding and which enable pupils to use skills effectively?

We can use data from the NCC project to see the underlying pattern of children's understanding of concepts of evidence in terms of the different stages of an investigation. The NCC project analysed checklist data on children's performance using 'criterion scores'. Briefly, the scores are cumulative in the sense that they are a measure of how far the pupil succeeded along successive stages of the investigation. Type 2 investigations (a single continuous independent variable), for example, were divided into eleven discrete steps. The first few are concerned with the identification of the correct variables and the design of a fair test. The middle section reflects the stages in the making of the appropriate measurements, while the end is concerned with the presentation and interpretation of the data.

When these scores are plotted for all type 2 investigations (Fig. 5.3), it is noticeable that there are two points where the percentage scores fall markedly, which in turn reflect the points at which pupils experience the most difficulty. The first point occurs at the design stage (steps 2–3), where pupils are required to identify the type and complexity of the variables. Once the variables have been identified, pupils are then able to carry out the investigation with some success until the second steep decline in the bar chart, which is at the data handling stage (steps 9–10), where pupils are required to represent the evidence in the form of a bar chart or line graph. It is evident that very few pupils are able to go on to the last stage of the investigation where they are required to generalise and evaluate appropriately.

The distributions for the other task types follow broadly the same pattern, except that in those tasks with categoric independent variables, the first point of decline does not occur. With this overall pattern in mind, we shall consider performance and procedural understanding under the four main headings of design, measurement, data handling and evaluation.

Design

Variable identification and the fair test

Both the APU and the NCC project found that most children, regardless of age, were able to design investigations so that the effect of the relevant independent variable could be investigated *somehow*. It is in the detail of *how* they did the investigation that the points of failure identified in the bar chart in Fig. 5.3 can be located.

The APU found that if there was more than one independent variable, then performance declined. In terms of control variables, the more 'obvious' the variables, the more likely they are to be controlled, especially when they are few in number. They also found that the effect of the substantive concept was particularly noticeable at the beginning of the investigation where the problem is defined by identifying the relevant variables. Lack of conceptual understanding caused some pupils to go astray.

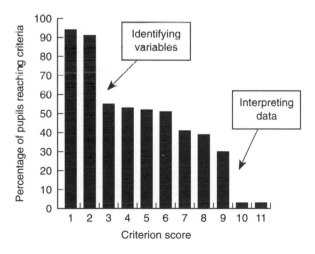

Fig. 5.3 Performance as measured by criterion scores on type 2 investigations

For example, in the NCC project, in an investigation where speed is the dependent and also a derived variable, identifying the correct components not unexpectedly caused problems. Pupils tended to pick one or other of the components of speed and even when they did measure both, they sometimes proceeded to use only one set of data, although of course, distance travelled is not a bad surrogate for speed if the variable is being used in a *qualitative* sense as 'faster than'. In the following example, Anna's group measured only the distance travelled.

Anna's group (Aged 12 – 13)

Does the speed of the model depend on the amount of energy stored in the elastic band?

How far pulled back	How far the butter tub travelled
2 cm	54 cm
4 cm	83 cm
6 cm	86 cm
8 cm	106.5 cm
10 cm	140 cm

We found out the speed of the model depends on the energy stored in the elastic band.

Table 5.1 shows the NCC data for the percentage of pupils who successfully identified the relevant variables for each of the types of tasks. (It should be noted that these data are drawn from individual checkpoints on the observation checklists rather than the criterion score.)

The data show that the vast majority of pupils understood the purpose of the task in that they recognised the appropriate independent and dependent variables. Where they did not, the effects of 'interesting' (for some reason) bits of apparatus sometimes caused distraction. In the example opposite, Steven's group was distracted by the presence of slotted weights in the classroom. They decided to vary the weights in the model, rather than the distance the elastic band was pulled back – a completely different investigation to the one they were asked to do.

The overall pattern (Table 5.1) is of a progressive decline in performance as the complexity of the task increases from type 1 to type 4. A task which is limited to one independent variable and one dependent variable causes few difficulties. The data suggest that pupils do not have difficulty deciding what the relevant variables are. This is perhaps not unexpected given that the tasks were largely well defined, or closed, in terms of defining the problem. Nevertheless, in type 4 tasks where there are two independent variables, pupils clearly still have some difficulty in their identification, the complexity of the design having defeated them. This trend is continued in the data associated with the control of variables, where 75 per cent of pupils controlled at least two variables in type 1 tasks, 51 per cent in type 3 tasks and 23 per cent in

Table 5.1 Identifying independent, dependent and control variables for types of tasks

Identification	Type 1	Type 2	Type 3	Type 4
Independent variable 1 identified correctly	98	94	83	71
Independent variable 2 identified correctly	n/a	n/a	87	67
Dependent variable identified correctly	98	93	89	92
At least 2 variables controlled	75	73	51	23

Steven (aged 12)

Find out how the distance moved by your model depends on the amount the elastic band is stretched.

What to do.

Attach an elastic band between the stool legs. Pull back and let go.

How far pulled back	How far it went	Weight inside
15 cm	3 m 30 cm	10 g
15 cm	3 m 68 cm	20 g
15 cm	3 m 29 cm	30 g

The results show how far it went and how many centimetres and metres.

Table 5.2 The identification of continuous variables

Identification	Type 1	Type 2	Type 3	Type 4
Independent variable defined as continuous	n/a	54	n/a	43
Dependent variable defined as continuous	98	93	89	92

type 4 tasks. The complexity of the design in types 3 and 4 frequently seems to mean that the relevant control variables are often ignored or overlooked. This is consistent with a general overload effect.

Variable types

We saw in Fig. 5.3 that the first point of difficulty children experience in type 2 investigations is in identifying the independent variable as *continuous*. The definition of 'continuous' in the data analysis centred on the use of at least three values of the independent variable. For the dependent variable, the definition need only rely on evidence that pupils had made a quantitative measurement. On these definitions, the percentage of pupils identifying both the independent and dependent variables as continuous are shown in Table 5.2.

Table 5.2 shows that a significant number failed to identify the *independent* variable as continuous when appropriate in type 2 and type 4 investigations, although they nearly all did so for the dependent variables. An example of this failure can be illustrated by considering the task: 'Find out how the temperature of the water affects how quickly the sugar dissolves.' Pupils would often choose to use 'hot' and 'cold' water, sometimes without measuring the temperature at all. Clearly, this categoric interpretation of the independent variable limits the extent to which the relationship between the independent and dependent variables can be explored.

To examine this point more closely, the percentage of pupils who identified the independent variable as continuous was broken down into specific tasks so that the concept associated *specifically with the independent variable* could be identified (Table 5.3).

Two issues emerge from these data. First, Table 5.3 shows that distance is an 'easier' substantive concept to identify as a continuous variable than temperature. This might be expected in view of the fact that children are more familiar with the skills of using rulers and tape measures and the language of length and height than they are with using thermometers and degrees. Another contributory pragmatic factor may be that length or height is simply easier and quicker to measure, while measuring temperature takes longer. Pupils may therefore decide to take the easy option and identify temperature as categoric – hot and cold – rather than measuring, if they think this is sufficient to answer the question.

Second, while the concept of distance was used in several tasks, it was particularly noticeable that where it referred to the pulling back of an elastic band to launch a model car (the forces and motion task), children found defining this sort of length as a continuous variable much easier than distance in the other investigations (Table 5.3). This may be explained by the fact that the other investigations involved a more 'static' kind of length, such as the length of a plank. By contrast, in the forces and motion task, pupils physically

pulled back the elastic band so that they were in control of its change and could see it 'in action' as a continuous variable.

If we turn to the nature of the *dependent* variable, however, the picture changes. Table 5.4 shows how the percentage of pupils identifying the nature of the dependent variable as continuous is high for all the substantive concepts in the sample. Temperature is noticeably easier for pupils to define as continuous than it was as an independent variable, although it is still lower than the other quantities. The reason for this changed picture could be related to the intrinsic role of the dependent variable. Since the dependent variable responds 'automatically' to the value of the independent variable, there is no need for the pupil to actively choose values. Pupils therefore do not need positively to apply the idea of a continuous variable.

The 'fair test'

We noted in Table 5.1 that the ability to control variables decreased as the complexity of the task rose. But there are other factors which influence the control element of a fair test. The more 'obvious' the variable, the more likely it is to be controlled, even to the extent that everything in sight is controlled as a ritual, rather than in a thoughtful way. Some variables to be controlled are not at all visible. For instance, in the heat task,

Table 5.3 The effect of different substantive concepts on identifying an independent variable as continuous

Independent variable	Percentage of pupils identifying variable as continuous
Temperature	41
Distance (in all investigations)	60
Distance (in forces and motion tasks only)	74

Table 5.4 The effect of different substantive concepts on identifying a dependent variable as continuous

Dependent variable	Percentage of pupils identifying variable as continuous
Distance (in all investigation)	77
Temperature	78
Time	81
Voltage	88
Distance (in forces and motion tasks only)	91

pupils have to measure the rate of loss of heat in the two containers whose insulation they are comparing. That comparison should, theoretically, be done at exactly the same temperature, since the rate of loss of heat depends on the instantaneous temperature difference between the contents of the container and its surroundings. Very few pupils seem to have controlled this temperature as a conscious act.

The evidence suggests that the notion of a 'fair test' is well established by the time children reach secondary school; it certainly merits a good deal of attention in primary science. But it is doubtful if the connection between a fair test and the validity of the resulting data is well understood. It is in just such instances that the importance of the synthesis of concepts of evidence becomes apparent.

Sample size and variation

The APU survey included an investigation about woodlice, described in Table 3.2. In designing the investigation, pupils have to decide how many woodlice to use in each trial or over a number of trials. Over half the pupils at age 15 used more than five woodlice in each trial, about a third used between two and five and less than a tenth used one woodlouse at a time (Driver *et al.*, 1984). It appears, therefore, that at the age of 15, choosing an appropriate sample size is still a problem for a significant number of pupils.

In summary, the research points to the conclusion that pupils experience little difficulty in the most basic part of the design of investigations, but that they do have difficulty in recognising the advantages of interpreting the independent variable as continuous and in understanding the consequences of this decision for the investigation as a whole. It is here that the sudden drop in performance (on the criterion score bar chart: Fig. 5.3) manifests itself. Choosing an appropriate sample size is also a problem for many pupils.

It seems that a number of individual concepts of evidence, particularly the notion of a continuous variable, are causing problems which relate in this example to the difficulties noted in the earlier section about pupils' use of measuring instruments

and graphs. If the very idea that a quantity can take on *any value* and that this value is connected to how that quantity behaves in the real world is not well understood, then the advantages of quantitative data will not be apparent. Over and above these individual factors, any increase in complexity of an investigation lowers performance as pupils start to lose track of the whole task.

Substantive concepts intrude most obviously and directly in the ability to *define* the appropriate dependent variable and to *recognise* that a variable must be controlled.

Measurement

Concepts of measurement refer not to the skill of measurement itself but to the decisions that have to be made concerning measurement. These include decisions about what instrument to choose (the most appropriate forcemeter for the task in hand, for instance), over what range and interval, when and how often to measure, and consideration of the need to repeat measurements.

The results of the NCC research tell us that children in primary schools (Key Stages 1 and 2) seem generally reluctant to measure, even though they are capable of using measuring instruments. At these key stages, only 30 per cent of children used measurement in investigations (Foulds *et al.*, 1992). Even at secondary school level, a significant number of pupils continued to judge changes in qualitative terms (34 per cent at age 11 and 13 per cent at age 13). In discussing the issue of measurement, Foulds *et al.* write (in relation to a sample of primary school children):

> It would seem that the use of measurement except where the question might explicitly specify the need is arbitrary at best, non-existent at worst. …We can only conclude that this aspect of investigative work is one which has not been grasped, for whatever reasons…

In an APU 'circus' practical (where pupils visit different stations to perform a variety of tasks), children were asked to use measurement when making observations, relationships and predictions.

Suzanne (Aged 12)

Which cup would be best for keeping drinks hot?

Time (min).	Bronze tin	Tin can	Polystyrene	Plastic	Plastic beaker	Glass B
0	**88°C**	**88**	**88**	**88**	**88**	**88**
1	78	78	86	84	82	82
2	75	76	84	80.5	80	79
3	74	74.5	81.5	77.5	76.5	76
4	71	71	79	75	75	73
5	**69**	**67.5**	**77.5**	**73**	**73.5**	**71**
Temp. went down by	**19°C**	**20.5**	**10.5**	**15**	**14.5**	**17**

At age 12, only one-fifth used measurement voluntarily except in a task (toy cars) in which they were heavily cued to do so (Archenhold *et al.*, 1989). The APU research also suggests that children's ability to handle measurements of length and temperature differ (Dickson *et al.*, 1984; Archenhold *et al.*, 1991; Foulds *et al.*, 1992) – temperature being the more difficult, as we noted above.

The example above shows an *inappropriate* use of the measurement of time and temperature in a heat transfer investigation. Investigations concerning heat loss seem to trigger a particular response in some pupils, who associate this kind of investigation with cooling curves regardless of whether or not this is appropriate. Perhaps they have been impressed by the unusual boredom of waiting for something to cool down, the laboratory equivalent of watching paint dry. Suzanne's table above illustrates the problem. Only the first and last measurements of temperature (shown in bold print in the table) are necessary to answer the question. The notion of scale is also relevant here in that five minutes is clearly not long enough to give any sort of reliable results.

Foulds *et al.* (1992) analysed the investigations in the NCC project in terms of whether children had used an appropriate scale. They defined scale as the carrying out of investigations 'in a manner which approximates sensible conditions and quantities'. The results show a clear progression with age and experience (Table 5.5).

In terms of *accuracy*, Foxman *et al.* (1990), reporting on the APU findings in mathematics, concluded that in performing measuring tasks accuracy may be associated in part with the pupil's perception of the 'expected' accuracy. There was a considerable change between the ages of 11 and 15 years in the accuracy with which pupils measured a straight line. At age 11, 61 per cent measured a line

Table 5.5 Percentage of pupils using scale and accuracy appropriately (Foulds *et al.*, 1992)

	Scale	Accuracy
Age 11 (Year 7)	58	76
Age 12 (Year 8)	69	73
Age 13 (Year 9)	79	78

of 130 mm to within 1 mm. At age 15, when presented with a similar task, 94 per cent measured the line to within 1 mm. In terms of science, the concept of *appropriate* accuracy is fundamental. There is, for instance, rarely a need to measure time to three decimal places, although pupils with digital watches often do so (constrained by the numbers on the watch or not familiar with the idea of rounding decimals perhaps?).

In terms of the range of readings, Strang (1990), in reporting on an APU task in which children were asked to find out how quickly the water coming out of the spout of a tea urn depends on the level of the water in the urn, found that almost half (42 per cent) of the 13-year-olds who did the task did not appreciate the importance of using an adequate *range* of levels.

Only a very small percentage of children *repeat* measurements in investigations. In the forces and motion investigation in the NCC project (see Table 4.3), where repeating measurements could very easily have been carried out and where it was clearly necessary, only six out of a sample of more than 250 children did so.

All these points rely, ultimately, on the pupils' ability to appreciate the idea of 'believable' data. It is only with this goal in mind, that the need for *appropriate* accuracy and range and *appropriate* repeats of measurements have any meaning over and above the algorithms of 'as accurate as possible', and 'always repeat things three times and average'. Unless and until pupils gain an understanding of validity and reliability of the evidence, they will, quite understandably, regard these issues as just 'one of those strange things that you do in science'. Indeed, it is only in the context of the whole task that these particular concepts of evidence can be seen to have meaning.

Given those reservations, most pupils, as we saw in the criterion score bar chart, make a reasonable attempt at taking measurements. It is only when we stand back and look at those measurements in the light of how 'believable' they are when interpreted, that we see that there is a real problem underneath the apparent success. Data handling is the subject of the next section.

Data handling

Once children have taken some measurements, how do they then go on to use them in the investigation? In terms of *recording* data, the APU found that at the age of 11, children's recording of data was frequently disorganised and descriptive with very little use of tables, even though their work in other categories showed that they were able to construct tables (Russell *et al.*, 1988). In the NCC project, an average of 68 per cent of all secondary pupils used tables to record their data.

The example overleaf taken from the NCC data shows a good use of tabulation in the 'fruits' investigation. David's conclusion, however, is a very parsimonious affair. This is a recurring feature of pupils' work; good basic presentation of data and inadequate interpretation.

It seems likely that pupils like David, with limited experience of investigative work, may not have been taught what is expected of them. They may well see the pattern in their results but not record it. The only clue that a fuller conclusion is required is the word 'how' in the question and this can easily be missed. David's conclusion may not reflect a lack of ability but a lack of appreciation of what is required.

If we consider the type 1 investigations in the NCC project (those with a single categoric independent variable), 72 per cent of children doing these investigations used a table. Although a bar chart is the most appropriate form of representation for type 1 investigations, it serves only as a form of display so it is not essential for the purpose of interpretation or generalisation. So, viewed in this way, it could be said that type 1 investigations can be adequately represented by a table. Indeed, Table 5.6 shows that only 11 per cent of children drew a bar chart, with 5 per cent drawing a line graph.

Looking back at the criterion scores in Fig. 5.3 for type 2 investigations (those with a single continuous independent variable), we noted that the second significant point of difficulty is where the children who have progressed successfully in the investigation, are required to *represent their data*

David (Aged 13)

Find out how the distance between the metal electrodes affects the voltage using different fruits.

We took an orange and wired it up to the voltage meter. We done this three time at different places on the orange. We recorded the results, e.g. the metal electrodes were 1 cm apart, the voltage was 6. We done this with the lemon and apple.

Fruit	cm apart	Voltage
apple	3.7 cm	4.5
apple	5.5 cm	4.0
apple	6.4 cm	3.9

Fruit	cm apart	Voltage
lemon	1.7 cm	6.2
lemon	3.1 cm	5.6
lemon	3.8 cm	5.4

Fruit	cm apart	Voltage
orange	1.7 cm	2.1
orange	3.8 cm	1.8
orange	3.1 cm	1.9

Yes the distance between metal electrodes does affect the voltage.

graphically before proceeding to use their evidence to support a final conclusion or generalisation. In type 2 investigations, a line graph is the most appropriate form of representation. Ideally, sufficient data should be collected to show any pattern between the independent and dependent variables. The representation here serves a much more important role than in type 1 investigations, in that while it is still a form of display, it can also reveal the nature of the pattern of the relationship between the variables. This is particularly the case with complex data or data where the line 'flattens

Table 5.6 Percentage scores for each investigation type

	Type 1	Type 2	Type 3	Type 4
Bar chart	11	18	4	4
Line graph	5	4	3	9

off', but even with linear relationships a line graph can serve a predictive function.

The APU found that very few 11-year-olds and only 10 per cent of 13-year-olds represented their data graphically, despite the fact that these children performed well on constructing graphs when this was assessed as an isolated activity (Strang, 1990). The choice of graph type was also often a problem.

It can be seen from Table 5.6 that in the NCC project, very few children actually chose to use a line graph for continuous data. Those that did, did not always do so in the most appropriate way. For instance, more pupils used a line graph for type 1 investigations, where it is not appropriate, than in type 2, where it clearly is appropriate.

An example of failure to represent data appropriately is shown on page 78. Paul and Craig collected data eminently suitable for a line graph. But their inappropriate choice of a bar chart was exacerbated by a decision to treat the x-axis as a set of labels, as if the values were of no greater significance than categories such as 'red' or 'big'. They also plotted the data inaccurately. Their conclusion was a repetition of their results with no awareness of a pattern or any attempt to generalise. They seem to have no understanding of the *pattern* representing the reality of the movement of their model.

Data collection and representation can take on an air of desperation on occasions. Reasons of space only dictate this choice of a relatively restrained approach to the cooling cups problem. In the investigation which Zoey recorded (p. 79), only the temperature readings in bold type were necessary. Zoey's group appears to have lost sight of the task – they seem to have carried out measurements in a ritualistic way. The drawing of three separate graphs also seems unnecessary and positively unhelpful in view of the fact that the conclusion that Zoey arrives at is incorrect and not informed by the data.

A similar effect was found with the bending beams task, to the extent that numerous tables and graphs of weight and sag appeared for nine or more 'planks', leading to a conclusion which reflected a failure of memory as to what the objectives of the investigation had been in the first place.

When it comes to *interpreting the patterns in graphs*, the APU reported that most children found it difficult to describe and use (read off, predict) patterns in graphs presented in written tests, though this improved with age (Taylor and Swatton, 1990). Austin *et al* (1991), again reporting on the APU findings, found that children of 12 and 14 years tended to bypass the data and draw on preconceived ideas. There was a tendency to impose patterns on ambiguous data, though it was noted that suspension of judgement is probably not encouraged in classroom science.

The NCC report also found that the inability to use data persists even when children collect their own data:

> ...*no pupils* referred to, or made use of their display work at any stage. Patterns which were apparent in the display were not recognised; irregularities in the sequenced results were not recognised...The overriding impression obtained whilst reviewing the reports was that pupils see the production of some form of graphical display as little other than a ritualistic exercise (something 'you do' after practical work) without recognising any purpose or significance in what they do.
>
> (Foulds *et al.*, 1992)

Austin *et al.* (1991) suggest that ordering data is a necessary first step towards generalisation, since unordered data are difficult to handle. By 14 years of age, more children ordered the data, but this was no guarantee they would then make a generalisation. Austin *et al.* also suggest that numerical data can be distracting in that children do not always link the data to the reality of the phenomenon that they represent, and so they may just repeat the numbers in their conclusions when they are asked what they have found out (as in the Paul and Craig example, see p. 78).

Paul and Craig (Aged 11)

Find out how the distance moved by the model depends on the amount the elastic band is stretched.

We had to find out the stretch of the elastic band made the butter tub went the longest. We put the elastic band on two chair legs and pulled it back and we let it go the best it was the one we pull back 30 cm it went four metres twenty six cm the one that went the least was the one we pulled back 5 cm it went 30 cm. It was a fear test because we used the same tub and the same elastic band.

How far we pulled it back	*How far it went*
25 cm	3 m 10 cm
20 cm	3 m 40 cm
15 cm	2 m 22 cm
10 cm	1 m 19 cm
30 cm	4 m 26 cm
5 cm	31 cm

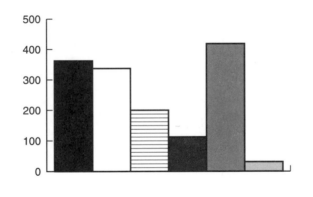

In another example from the NCC project, Paul, Mark and Stephen (see p. 80) produced a good table of data. They had ordered their results and reported a generalised pattern at the start of their written record. It seems that they then decided that a bar chart might be a good thing. They then drew one which, one could be forgiven for thinking, was a deliberate attempt to confuse the reader. Why they chose to shuffle the order of their x-axis is left to the reader as an exercise in imagination. It appears from the bar chart that, to this group, the values of the stretch of the elastic band are little more than labels bearing no relationship to each other. Their conclusion was clearly not based on the pattern in their bar chart.

Zoey (Aged 12)

Which cup kept water hottest?

Type of cup	Start temp.	After 1 min.	After 2 min.	After 3 min.	After 4 min.	After 5 min.	How much temp. dropped
Polystyrene	**88°C**	82°C	79°C	76°C	73°C	**70°C**	**18°C**
Plastic	**70°C**	64°C	62°C	60°C	58°C	**58°C**	**12°C**
Paper	**75°C**	72°C	70°C	65°C	62°C	**60°C**	**15°C**

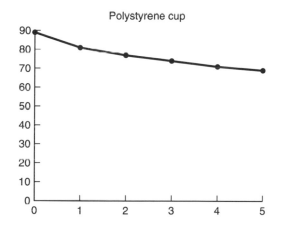

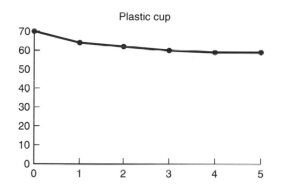

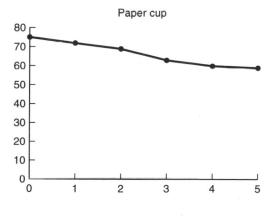

Our conclusion is that of the three cups the paper cup is the best as from its starting temperature it dropped the least amount

Paul, Mark and Stephen (Aged 11)

Find out how the distance moved by the model depends on the amount the elastic band is stretched.

What we found: What we found was the further you pull the elastic band back the tube went further.

Stretched (cm)	
2	40.1 cm
4	66 cm
6	133.5 cm
8	250.8 cm
10	237 cm
12	250 cm
14	361.5 cm
16	400 cm
18	537 cm
20	547 cm

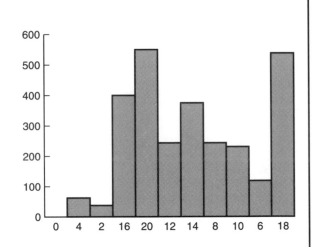

Another group produced similar data but chose to order their bar chart:

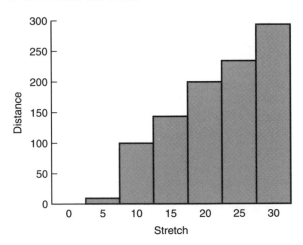

and then concluded: 'The further the elastic band is pulled the faster the model moves across the floor.'

This group appears to be moving towards the recognition of a pattern but have not yet realised that a line graph would illustrate the pattern better.

Foulds *et al.* (1992) wrote that while the majority of children attempted a conclusion, the conclusions 'were not in keeping with the data at all, but were, in fact, at odds with it'. And also: 'Many of their conclusions and inferences made little, if any, use of the data which had been gathered.' We have seen a number of instances of the latter in examples earlier in this chapter.

Does the *type* of investigation affect children's ability to make sense of the investigation? Table 5.7 shows the percentage scores for 'sensible' generalisations for each investigation type. (Our definition of 'generalisation' was liberally applied; if we had required the generalisation to be both true *and* founded on the data, the figures would have been very much lower.) The overall trend is that the per-

Table 5.7 Percentage scores for generalisation for each investigation type

	Type 1	Type 2	Type 3	Type 4
Appropriate generalisation	53	36	33	25

centage score decreases as the investigation type increases. As would be expected, type 1 investigations are the easiest from which to generalise, with over half the sample generalising appropriately. As the complexity of the data increases, so the interpretation of the data becomes increasingly difficult.

The example below of a type 2 investigation shows only the graph produced (from a table) by 'Group A', who measured speed by measuring the distance the butter tub travelled in one second. Their generalisation is tied to an understanding of the concepts underlying the task or to the ability to link the variables and the data to the reality

that they represent. It could be that such an understanding is necessary before the notion of the pattern in the data becomes meaningful. Only then, perhaps, can we expect to see the transition from a disorganised bar chart (Paul, Mark and Stephen, aged 11), through an organised one to the line graph below.

In type 3 and type 4 investigations, where multivariate data are involved, neither bar charts nor line graphs are particularly helpful. Similar percentages of pupils chose to represent their data graphically as in the other types of investigations, supporting the above observation that the drawing of any type of graph may be a ritual rather than a purposeful exercise. Incidences of success were few and far between here. So, rather than list them, we have included two examples of pupils' work which show how well they *can* do. Simon's final conclusion may be open to question, but there can be little doubt that this is a good piece of work from an 11-year-old pupil.

Group A

Does the speed of the model depend on the amount of energy stored in the elastic band

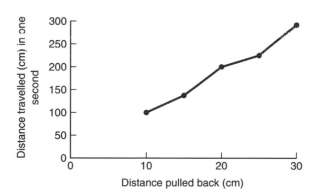

The energy in the elastic band does affect the speed of the carton. The more energy in elastic band, the faster the carton goes.

Simon *(age 11)*

The great tea problem

I am doing the one to find out whether both things affect how quickly the sugar dissolves

First I filled a beaker with hot water and made sure it was 75 ml, then I put 10 spatulafulls in and see the timer going simultaneously. I did the same again but put cold water in instead of hot water. After that I put some hot water in and put white sugar in instead of brown, then I put cold water in instead of hot water. I also stirred them all.

Type of sugar	Temperature of water (°C)	Time for sugar to dissolve (min:s)
Brown	20	3:46
White	21	1:46
Brown	72	1:07
White	75	1:00

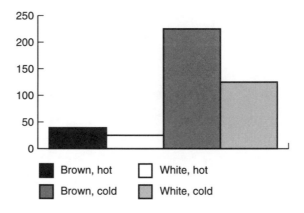

■ Brown, hot   □ White, hot

▨ Brown, cold   ▨ White, cold

They both make a difference but sugar doesn't matter as much as the water.

Brent *(age 11)*

In this experiment I set up the apparatus as shown in the diagram. I then changed the distance between the two strips of metal and observed any change in the reading of the voltmeter. I then repeated the experiment this time keeping the distance apart constant and varying the depths of the strips in the fruit (a lemon) and measured the reading. My results are displayed in the table and graphs opposite.

Distance between	Volts
5	2.6
4	2.7
3	2.8
2	2.9
1	3.6

Amount submerged	Volts
5 cm	4.5
4 cm	3.9
3 cm	3.7
2 cm	3.6

My conclusion is that the greater proportion of the plate submerged and the closer together (without touching) the higher the voltage will be.

Graph to show varying voltage due to changing distance between poles

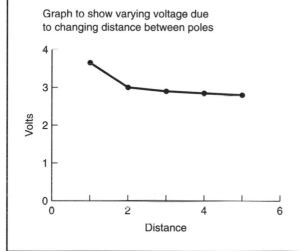

Graph to show varying voltage due to changing depth between poles

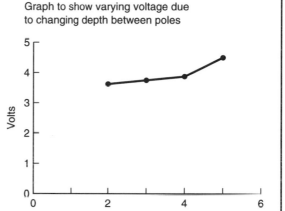

The overall picture, then, is that in general children experience considerable difficulty in interpreting graphical information and indeed in interpreting data overall. Again, we are driven to the view that it is the underlying understanding of the purpose of gathering data, and the role that evidence plays in the work of science, that is conspicuous by its absence. This is not surprising, and indeed it may be asking too much of pupils of this age to expect them to cope with these ideas. But until we have tried teaching these ideas, we shall not know. What can be said is that there are enough instances of pupils' work which do show elements of that understanding to give us hope that systematic teaching will result in considerable improvement.

Evaluation

What do we know about children's understanding of the validity and reliability of an investigation? There is very little direct research evidence concerning these concepts. This may be because they are in practice very difficult to probe.

In an early APU report (Harlen *et al.*, 1981), 11-year-olds were assessed as to their 'willingness to be critical of procedures used'. This was based on observation by the assessor and on the pupils' answers to a question after the investigation about what changes they would make if they did the investigation again. Clearly, the question itself prompts the pupil to evaluate. The resulting data (Table 5.8) are difficult to interpret given that Harlen *et al*. admit that in some investigations where the pupils had performed satisfactorily, the only alternative to consider was a less satisfactory procedure. In these cases, there was no need for a pupil to be critical of his or her work.

In the NCC project, less than 1 per cent of the total sample attempted any form of evaluation. This may well reflect a different definition of the term. We are defining evaluation in this book as that underlying understanding which guides the design of the complete task. Other workers have required a more explicit indication of the understanding of evaluation by relying on pupils to spot errors in their procedures.

This evidence, however, is retrospective. Asking pupils to comment on how they think they could improve their investigation is already too late. What we are concerned with here is the ability to keep the requirements of believable (that is, valid and reliable) evidence in mind throughout the task – from defining variables so that the question is being answered, to choosing appropriate ranges of instruments and readings to spot patterns unambiguously, to seeing the link between the data and the type of graphical representation, right through to the critical inter- pretation of both data and method of data collec- tion. What we have seen is that this notion is at best patchy and at worst non-existent.

They are difficult ideas. Some would argue that they are more appropriate to sixth-form level (17- and 18-year-olds) or higher, and certainly the mathematical treatment of errors is notoriously difficult for pupils at A level. But lower-level notions of validity and reliability are, we believe, achievable. Work in some local schools certainly supports that belief, but it also highlights the fact that sorting out the best techniques of teaching is not going to be easy.

Summary

In this chapter, we have used existing research data to apply the notion of concepts of evidence to children's performance in investigations. We have shown that children's procedural under- standing of the *design* are generally good in that they can structure the investigation successfully, but that children do experience difficulty in identi- fying variables as continuous where appropriate. Secondary pupils have a reasonable grasp of the *measurement*, although they seldom repeat mea- surements. Ideas about *data handling* and *evaluation* are particularly poor. Foulds *et al*. (1992) wrote: 'During analysis of children's work it became very clear that this area of children's working [the use of data and evaluation] appeared to be severely neglected', and 'The most striking feature of pupils' work is their lack of understand- ing of the nature of evidence.'

We would wish to suggest that, harking back to our procedural taxonomy, while the individual skills and concepts of evidence are being dealt with in teaching to some extent, the ideas of appli- cation and, in particular, synthesis, are less to the fore. We need examples of schemes of work which integrate these ideas successfully and which develop a common language of discourse between both teachers and pupils. As we argued above, unless the link between the design and implemen- tation of an investigation and the requirements of believable evidence are dealt with, pupils will tend to 'go through the motions' in practical lessons.

Table 5.8 The APU assessment of pupil attitudes

Category	Percentage of pupils
Uncritical of procedures used	41
Aware of alternative procedures but does not have very good reasons for suggesting changes	38
Shows awareness of variables not controlled, the need to repeat measurements, ineffective procedures or factors central to investigation	20

All of which points inescapably to improvements in teaching and in schemes of work to take these ideas into account. And it is to issues of teaching that we now turn.

References

Archenhold, F., Austin, R., Bell, J., Black, P., Braund, M., Daniels, S., Holding, B., Russell, A. and Strang, J. (1991). *Profiles and Progression in Science Exploration*. Assessment Matters No. 5. London, SEAC/EMU.

Austin, R., Holding, B., Bell, J. and Daniels, S. (1991). *Patterns and Relationships in School Science*. Assessment Matters No. 7. London, SEAC/EMU.

Dickson, L., Brown, M. and Gibson, O. (1984). *Children Learning Mathematics: A Teacher's Guide to Recent Research*. Eastbourne, Holt, Rinehart and Winston for the Schools Council.

Driver, R., Child, D., Gott, R., Head, J., Johnson, S., Worsley, C. and Whyte, F. (1984). *Science in Schools: Age 15*. APU Science Report for Teachers No. 2. London, HMSO.

Foulds, K., Gott, R. and Feasey, R. (1992). *Investigative Work in Science*. Durham, University of Durham.

Foxman, D., Ruddock, G. and McCallum, I. (1990). *APU Mathematics Monitoring, 1984–88 (Phase 2)*. Assessment Matters No. 3. London, SEAC/EMU.

Gott, R. (1984). *Electricity at Age 15*. APU Science Report for Teachers No. 7. London, HMSO.

Harlen, W., Black, P. and Johnson, S. (1981). *Science in Schools: Age 11*. APU Science Report for Teachers No. 1. London, HMSO.

Russell, T., Black, P., Harlen, W., Johnson, S. and Palacio, D. (1988). *Science at Age 11: A Review of APU Findings, 1980–84*. London, HMSO.

Strang, J. (1990). *Measurement in School Science*. Assessment Matters No. 2. London, SEAC/EMU.

Taylor, R.M. and Swatton, P. (1990). *Graph Work in School Science*. Assessment Matters No. 1. London, SEAC/EMU.

Welford, G., Harlen, W. and Schofield, B. (1985). *Practical Testing at Ages 11, 13 and 15*. APU Science Report for Teachers No. 6. London, HMSO.

CHAPTER 6

Investigations and teaching

Introduction

In the light of the research presented in the last two chapters, how can investigations best be incorporated into the science curriculum? We have suggested that one of the ultimate aims of the science curriculum is to enable as many pupils as possible to recall, understand, apply and synthesise (1) a whole range of skills and concepts of evidence *as well as* (2) the 'traditional' or substantive concepts of science to solve a range of problems. To achieve these aims, teachers need gradually to expose pupils to a range of increasingly more complex concepts *and* procedures.

How can investigations help in achieving these curricular goals? We considered the roles of different types of practical work in Chapters 1 and 2 and from this suggested that investigations are the best type of practical to provide children with the opportunity to *synthesise* procedural understanding, which in turn relies on their understanding of concepts of evidence.

What we must explore is how investigations can best be selected to develop that range of skills and procedural understanding which underpins this area of science. In this chapter, we shall consider first how investigations can be designed to focus on a specific learning outcome. And, second, we shall put forward some ideas for reinforcing particular concepts of evidence and then examine the issues of progression and differentiation.

Changing the overall focus of investigations

The procedural and conceptual understanding used in investigations cannot be separated because they are inextricably intertwined; procedures in science cannot be employed without using concepts and likewise concepts cannot be used without employing procedures. However, we can emphasise one or the other of these two types of understanding by carefully manipulating the structure of the investigation. Foulds *et al.* (1992) give some examples of how this can be done (Table 6.1). The examples are restricted to the quantitative investigations described in previous chapters.

The investigations in column 1 might be used when pupils are beginning investigative work. They use relatively simple concepts and the procedural understanding required includes basic measuring skills together with ideas of a fair test, range, interval and patterns. By contrast, the investigations in the second column, which involve two independent variables, require an increasingly systematic application of procedural understanding. The evidence that has to be collected, interpreted and evaluated is more complex, since it involves multivariate data. The concepts involved, however, remain relatively straightforward.

The third column gives examples of investigations where the conceptual demand is higher, in that the identification of the variables requires more advanced knowledge and understanding. The variables may also be derived quantities as in the case of speed. This increases the sophistication of

Table 6.1 Changing the emphasis of investigations (based on Foulds *et al.*, 1992)

Low procedural understanding / *Low* conceptual understanding	*High* procedural understanding / *Low* conceptual understanding	*Low* procedural understanding / *High* conceptual understanding	*High* procedural understanding / *High* conceptual understanding
Find out whether sugar dissolves faster in hot water than in cold water	Find out whether the rate at which sugar dissolves depends on: (a) the type of sugar, and (b) the temperature of the solution	Find out which of these chemicals cause hardness in water	Find out how the speed of the thiosulphate reaction depends on: (a) the concentration of the solutions and (b) the temperature
Find out how the distance travelled by a toy car depends on the amount the elastic is wound up	Find out how the distance travelled by a model car depends on: (a) its weight, and (b) the force used to get it moving	Find out whether the speed of a model dragster depends on the amount of energy stored in the elastic band	Find out how the efficiency of an electric motor depends on: (a) the load being lifted, and (b) the speed at which it is operated
Find out whether plants grow better if they are watered with fertiliser solution than if they are just given ordinary water	Find out how the growth of a plant depends on: (a) the amount of light which strikes it, and (b) the temperature of the surroundings	Find out how the rate at which fermentation takes place depends on the temperature of the solution	Find out how the rate at which photosynthesis takes place depends on: (a) the light intensity, and (b) the temperature

the evidence without necessarily increasing its volume. The investigations in the fourth column are examples where both the procedural and conceptual demands are high.

Targeting specific concepts of evidence within whole investigations

It is tempting to think that carrying out an investigation *requires* that pupils be taught skills and concepts of evidence in advance and, as far as is possible, one by one. But this inductive approach is at least a debatable one. Most concepts of evidence are closely tied to whole investigations, so that it is difficult to teach them individually.

Consider the notion of the relative scale of the variables in a practical: the choosing of sensible proportions for the relevant variables in relation to the instruments available. Let us consider a simple situation, such as finding out which of several kinds of paper towel is most effective in soaking up water. If pupils attempted to measure the amount of water soaked up in one square centimetre of paper towel, most people would agree that this would be an inappropriate scale, since the relative amounts of water soaked up by such a small area would be difficult to measure using the measuring instruments which are normally available in schools. Clearly, it is difficult to convey this idea of scale without describing the whole investigation of which it is a part. Again, if we consider the idea of 'believability' of evidence, it is necessary, at least until the notion is embedded, to address the issue in the context of data that pupils have collected themselves and, therefore, 'understand'. We can also draw on our own experience and the experience of other teachers in the area, which suggest that lessons which develop skills and concepts of evidence *within* investigative work, with the skills set clearly within the context of a whole investigation, are seen as more meaningful by the pupils.

So the order should be to teach whole but carefully focused investigations first. These should then be followed up by exercises on specific skills and concepts of evidence to teach or reinforce specific points of difficulty which have become apparent in the investigation. This order of teaching may not be easy to organise, but we believe it is necessary to avoid 'fragmentation'.

In the following section, we suggest ways of targeting each of the broad categories of concepts of evidence, design, measurement, data handling and evaluation, all within investigations. These investigations, together with the follow-up activities, will then constitute a menu to be drawn on in the design of schemes of work considered in the next chapter.

Design

The identification of variables (as independent and dependent).	Example: Which fuel is best?

Any simple investigation where a variable is not specified can be used to focus on the identification of variables. The lesson could begin for instance with a brainstorming session on what 'best' means, either directly with the whole class or after small group discussion. A simple planning exercise before carrying out the investigation using both the task in hand and other examples can be used to reinforce the concept of independent and dependent variables.

The design of the fair test and its associated control variables.	Example: Which paper towel is best for mopping up water?

The choice of an investigation which involves several control variables can reinforce the importance of the fair test. Brainstorming can be used here too. A discussion of the effect of *not* controlling variables is also useful.

The type of variables (categoric, discrete or continuous).	Examples: Which type of insulation is best for lagging a central heating boiler? (independent categoric variable) How is heat loss affected by number of layers of insulation? (independent discrete variable) How does heat loss depend on the volume of the boiler? (independent continuous variable)

Types of variables can be emphasised by using a series of investigations such as the examples above, either sequentially with the whole class or by having different groups in the class doing different investigations. In the latter case, whole class discussion following the investigative work is essential to focus on and compare the different types of variables.

After the investigation, the relationship between the type of variable and the type of graph can be discussed. For instance, it may be helpful to relate the 'sudden jumps' in categoric variables to the appearance of the bar chart and the gradual change of continuous variables to the linear or curvilinear form of the line graph.

Sample size and variation.	Example: Find out how light affects the growth of cress seeds.

Sample size can be emphasised by any investigation where this concept plays a significant role, often in biological contexts. It may be useful to allow the investigation to proceed and then compare the 'believability' of the results of groups who have selected different sample sizes.

All these examples are dependent on the teacher focusing the practical on the relevant idea. Here group and/or class discussion at strategic points throughout the investigation are essential so that the aim of the lesson – to learn about design – is clear to all. The role of the teacher here is paramount, a factor which is discussed further in the next chapter.

Measurement

Concepts of evidence associated with scale.	Examples: Which paper towel is best for mopping up water? Find out how the rate of dissolving of (a chemical) depends on the temperature of the water.

The importance of relative scale can be a difficult concept to convey. The first of the examples above can be used to draw pupils' attention to the importance of matching the scale, of the amount of water that can be squeezed from the piece of paper, to the instrumentation available. A relatively coarse measuring cylinder, for instance, constrains the optimum size of the sample if the measurement is to be accurate enough. In the other example, the saturation of a solution is a concept which influences scale. Clearly, if too much chemical is used, the solution will become saturated. If this situation arises among groups in the course of the investigation, then by comparing results afterwards, the effect of inappropriate scale will become obvious.

Concepts of evidence associated with range and interval and the choice of instrument.	Example: Find out how the height of a slope affects the amount of pull needed to pull an object up it.

Investigations which involve continuous variables almost inevitably lead to considerations of the concepts of appropriate range and interval. The importance of range often becomes obvious when interpreting patterns in line graphs. If the range is too narrow, only part of the pattern will emerge; in the example above, for instance, the relationship is not linear but in fact peaks at an angle somewhat less than 90° due to the effects of friction. Again, whole class discussion of different groups' results is very useful here.

The concept of the choice of instrument can be emphasised by making available a wide variety of measuring instruments from which the pupils have to select. In the same investigation, a large number of forcemeters with different ranges should be made available as a prerequisite, if pupils are to understand the effect of their choice on the accuracy of their measurements. The teacher might allow pupils to choose inappropriately in order to learn from their mistakes or he or she may stop the class after groups have chosen their instrument and made their first few readings and elicit ideas from the children about the pros and cons of different forcemeters for the task.

Repeatability.	Example: Find out how the bounciness of the squash ball depends on temperature.

The need for repeatability can be targeted by using any investigation in which variability is a prominent feature. In the example, the need for repeats is essential if the evidence is to be reliable *and* accurate enough to uncover the trend in the results. Again, group comparisons can be useful after the investigation or, alternatively, the teacher can question groups while they are collecting their data in order to encourage them to consider the reliability of their measurements. The teacher might ask, for instance: 'If you did it again would you get the same results?'

Accuracy.	**Example:** Which sugar dissolves the quickest?

The appropriateness of a particular level of accuracy can be brought out by comparing the data from different groups in the class. For instance, in dissolving investigations pupils often record time with digital watches to three decimal places. Other groups may record the dissolving time to the nearest minute. The latter may not be accurate enough to reveal a trend but the former may be equally inappropriate.

Data handling

Concepts of evidence associated with data handling; the use of tables.	**Examples:** Which type of sugar dissolves quickest? How does the temperature of the water affect dissolving time?

The use of a table as a planner or organiser reflects an understanding of the design of the investigation in terms of the identification and the type of the variables. All too often it is used *after* data collection as a neat way of organising jottings in the backs of books. A table can show the intended number, range and interval of the values of the dependent variable. Two related investigations, one of which involves a categoric and the other a continuous independent variable, can serve to point to the advantages of a table as an advance organiser (Fig. 6.1).

It can be seen that the column headings identify the independent and dependent variables. In tables

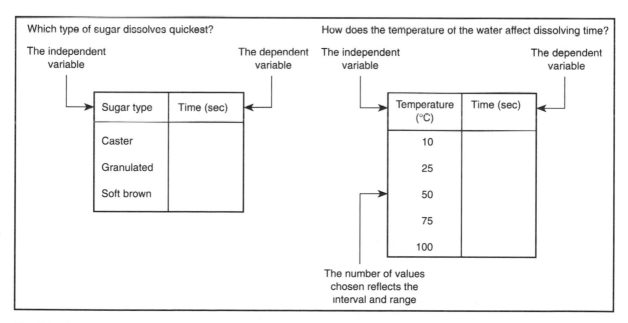

Fig. 6.1 The use of tables to structure and plan investigations

of continuous variables, the values chosen also set the number, range and interval of the readings. Concepts related to the type of variable, range and interval all come into play here; it is perhaps this interaction that causes pupils so many problems, with continuous data in particular. A table such as this, used as a discussion point on the blackboard, can serve as a very useful teaching aid in discussing the planning of investigations.

Graphs.	**Example:** Find out how the distance travelled (by the toy car) depends on the amount the elastic band is pulled back. When you have finished, you will be given a distance and asked to predict how far back to pull your elastic band.

The choice of graph type is related to the type of variable. For many pupils, graphs are simply a display, and the importance of line graphs as reflecting an underlying relationship between variables is missing. One way of approaching the issue is through an investigation where the line graph can be shown to be a positive advantage rather than a chore, as in the example above. This kind of competition which demands interpolation or extrapolation, encourages pupils to see the purpose of line graphs for exploring the relationship between two variables. Without such a purpose, the drawing of a line graph for continuous data can become a ritual.

The concept of patterns provides another opportunity to look at the pupils' ideas of the relationship between the data and the reality that they represent. Patterns in the data are usually determined by examining tables or graphical representation. Understanding how those patterns relates to the reality of the task in hand can be targeted by asking different groups to discuss what their data mean. Alternatively, if, in the second dissolving investigation (Fig. 6.1), the pupils are asked to predict from

their results what happens if, for instance, the temperature is doubled from 30 to 60°C, they may proceed to double (or halve) the dissolving time – that is, using *mathematical* patterns which do not relate to the *scientific* pattern of the variables.

Multivariate data.	**Examples:** Which cups should the market stall holder buy to keep drinks hot? Should he choose: • Plastic or polystyrene? • Cups with lids or with no lids? How does the sag of a plank depend on the weight on the plank and its length?

In the first example, the most efficient way of considering the effect of the two independent variables is as shown in Fig. 6.2. The research evidence shows that many children will tackle such investigations by testing the two independent variables separately. In the example given, pupils tend to test the effect of the type of cup and presence/absence of lid in two separate investigations. This investigation

	Starting temp.	Temp. after 10 min.	Temp. drop
Plastic cup (no lid)			
Plastic cup (with lid)			
Polystyrene cup (no lid)			
Polystyrene cup (with lid)			

Fig. 6.2 A multivariate table

could be made more realistic if the costs of the cups and lids are given to the pupils so that the relative effects of heat loss and cost can be assessed. Where the independent variables are continuous, as in the case of the second example above, two or more graphs drawn on the same axes can help to illustrate the relative effects.

Evaluation – reliability and validity

Children can be gradually introduced to these concepts by carrying out investigations where there is a target audience, perhaps others in the class. If groups are doing different tasks, each group can see the need for convincing other groups who have not 'seen' and therefore are not in a position to 'believe'. Choice of task here is less important, although one in which there is not a self-evidently correct answer is likely to be more fruitful. The slopes investigation mentioned above is one such task.

Techniques such as asking groups of pupils to defend their results against cross-examination by an advocate from another group, or the class, can be of use here. Such techniques require careful introduction and a sense of theatre to drive home the importance of the audience, which has to be convinced by the 'objective' evidence of the scientist. Gradually, pupils begin to realise that the nature of scientific evidence is not straightforward.

The reinforcement of concepts of evidence

We shall mention briefly here some ideas for reinforcement, most profitably used as a follow-up activities to targeted investigations.

Associated with design

The example of a question from a written exercise from CASE (Adey *et al.*, 1989), which focuses on the concept of *the fair test* and associated *control variables*, is shown here:

> During a school sports afternoon, it was decided to see if boys ran faster than girls. John and Jane were timed during this race, they both started to run at the same time.
> Is this a fair test?
> If not, why not?

CASE uses pictures and diagrams to help to clarify the question and also makes these exercises more attractive to the pupil.

Associated with measurement

These two follow-up activities were designed to follow on from a 'slopes' task ('Find out how the angle of the slope affects how easy it is to pull the brick up'). The first activity focuses on the choice of measuring instrument for a particular task (see Fig. 6.3). The second (Fig. 6.4) focuses on the idea of a continuous variable and, more particularly, on the notion of range, interval and number of a set of values for the independent variable.

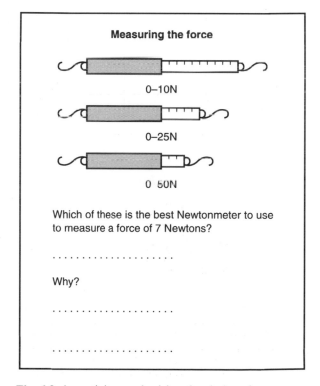

Fig. 6.3 An activity emphasising the choice of an appropriate measuring instrument

The pupils are asked to think about an investigation to find out how the angle of a slope affects how easy it is to pull a brick up.

Here are the tables from several groups

Group 1	Group 2	Group 3
10	0	0
30	30	10
70	60	20
90	90	30
		40
		50

Group 4	Group 5
0	0
5	20
15	40
20	60
40	80
45	
70	
90	

Which angles would you use?

Angle

Which group's is best?
....
Why?
....
Which group's is worst?
....
Why?
....

Fig. 6.4 An activity emphasising the choice of range and interval

Susan, Vicky and Leanne had made model cars using margarine tubs. To 'launch' the cars, they used elastic bands stretched across stools. They each measured how far the cars travelled. They put their results in a table.

They each drew a graph to show their results.

Amount elastic pulled back	Distance travelled
2 cm	35 cm
4 cm	55 cm
6 cm	70 cm
8 cm	87 cm
10 cm	101 cm

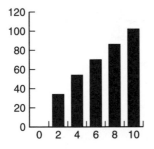 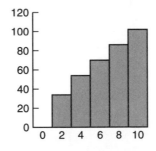 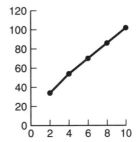

There was going to be a competition to see who could land their car closest to a line drawn on the floor.
They could measure how far it was from the elastic band to the line before they started.
1 The three graphs show the same results in different ways.
Which graph do you think is best? Explain why you chose this one.
2 Discuss with your friends which graphs *they* think are best.
When you have agreed which is the best, draw it onto a full sheet of paper. Remember that the labels are important.

Fig. 6.5 An activity concerning the choice of type of graph (based on an example in Foulds *et al.*, 1990)

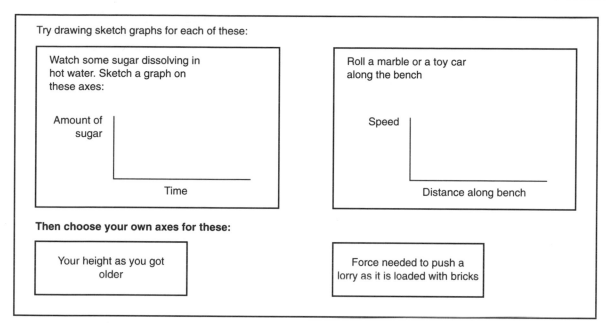

Fig. 6.6 Examples of a line graph exercise which can be used to teach the relationship between the behaviour of a variable and a graphical pattern

Associated with data handling

Understanding the reasoning which underlies the choice of graph type, with its link to the type of variable, can be approached using 'second-hand' data such as in Fig. 6.5. Developing the understanding of *patterns* in data is, as we have noted from the research, one of the more difficult concepts. One technique which works well is to use sketch graphs. Asking pupils to say which graph 'feels' like the stretching of a rubber band, for example, seems to help in establishing that link with reality that is so often missing. Some examples for follow-up activities are given in Fig. 6.6. After pupils have become familiar with the idea of sketch graphs, the teacher could ask pupils to predict before doing an investigation what the shape or pattern of the resulting graph might be.

Associated with evaluation

Evaluation is closely linked with a recognition that investigations rely on valid and reliable data. With older and more able children, recent press cuttings on topics such as the incidence of leukaemia around Sellafield or the testing of new drugs could form the basis of a class discussion aimed at introducing pupils to the idea that data can be presented which may be invalid, or unreliable in their accuracy or interpretation. Such exercises also help children to relate school science to the real world. With younger children, using data from other similar-aged children can be a good source of appropriate second-hand data.

Targeting conceptual understanding

Investigations can be useful at the beginning of a topic as a 'window' into children's implicit understanding. Sometimes pupils have an everyday understanding of an idea such as heat transfer or friction. Often those ideas are held implicitly. Sometimes they are wrong. Some examples of open investigations based on the research programme and used in this way are shown in Table 6.2.

Table 6.2 Examples of investigations which can uncover children's misconceptions

Investigation	Concept focus
Which fuel is best?	This investigation can be used as an introduction to the concept of fuels as concentrated sources of energy. The choice of the dependent variable includes: smoke, smell, time to heat water, amount of fuel to heat water. Each of these responses can be used to open up ideas concerned with environmental pollution, or the distinction between power output and total energy content.
Which materials would be best for a hedgehog to use for its nest?	This investigation can be used as an introduction to the concepts of heat transfer. An example of a pupil response is of interest here. One low-ability pupil asked for a hard-boiled egg to use as a hedgehog. He asked that it be hard-boiled for a long time. Eventually, it dawned on the teacher that he imagined that an egg could be packed with heat – a caloric theory view.

Table 6.3 Varying procedural demand within a single context

Investigation	Variable structure
Find out whether the amount of juice depends on the type of apple which is used	A single categoric independent variable
Find out how the amount of fruit juice extracted depends on the amount of pectinase enzyme which is used	A single continuous independent variable
Find out whether: (a) the type of enzyme used, or (b) the type of apple which is used has the greatest effect on the amount of fruit juice extracted from the pulp	Two categoric independent variables
Find out how the amount of fruit juice extracted depends on: (a) the amount of enzyme, and (b) the temperature of the pulp	Two continuous independent variables

Progression and differentiation by outcome

The structuring and sequencing of activities is the basis of well-planned schemes of work. Choosing investigations which gradually increase in their demand is just one element of that structure. Differentiation within a particular lesson relies on the same principle. So the same examples can be used in the one lesson, to enable pupils working at different levels of understanding to be challenged but not overwhelmed. We shall consider first how to structure the procedural demand, and second, the conceptual demand.

The procedural demands of investigations within the same context can be matched to pupils of different ability. Table 6.3 gives examples, within the context of juice extraction, of this differentiation by task. Using the same context means that the conceptual element can be kept the same while the procedural complexity is changed.

Foulds *et al.* (1992) point out that an investigation set at a high level of procedural demand can be

Table 6.4 Investigations with an increasing conceptual demand within one context

Find out whether the distance travelled depends on the amount by which the elastic band is stretched	Find out whether the distance travelled by the model depends on the amount of energy stored in the elastic band	Find out whether the average speed of the model depends on the force exerted by the elastic band	Find out whether the average speed of the model depends on the amount of energy stored in the elastic band

performed in practice at each of the lower levels with differentiation by outcome. For example, the investigation with two continuous independent variables could be restructured by pupils as having one rather than two categoric independent variables.

In the same way that procedural demand can be varied to meet the needs of differentiation and progression, so can conceptual demand. The examples in Table 6.4 show how investigations can be targeted so that the conceptual demand is low or high, while the procedural demand is kept relatively constant.

By making both the conceptual and procedural demands of an investigation high, as in the fourth column of Table 6.1, investigations can explore both conceptual and procedural understanding. These investigations make high demands on pupils However, the logic of our argument with regard to the overall aims of the science curriculum and using the research findings in Chapters 4 and 5, is that having developed an effective base of procedural and conceptual understanding, the pupil is then in a position to recognise when and where the various procedures are applicable.

Summary

In this chapter, we have shown how the understanding of concepts of evidence can be taught through carefully chosen investigations which hinge on particular concepts. Follow-up exercises, written or practical, can and should serve to reinforce the concept in another context, to begin the task of allowing pupils to *apply* the concept. As pupils' repertoire increases, so we can begin to widen the menu of investigations, allowing for tasks to be selected, within the same overall concept, for groups of pupils at different stages of procedural and conceptual understanding.

References

Adey, P., Shayer, M. and Yates, C. (1989). *Thinking Science: The Materials of the CASE Project.* Walton-on-Thames, Nelson.

Foulds, K., Mashiter, J. and Gott, R. (1990). *Investigations in Science.* Glasgow, Blackie.

Foulds, K., Gott, R. and Feasey, R. (1992). *Investigative Work in Science.* Durham, University of Durham.

CHAPTER 7

Incorporating investigations into a scheme of work

One school in the North-East has been developing schemes of work incorporating investigations for some time. What follows is part of a discussion with the school on how to teach for procedural understanding and the difficulties of devising schemes of work.

Investigations do need to be specifically targeted – but not in the 'follow this instruction', teacher's way. The teacher has to be aware of the concepts of evidence they are trying to develop and give them practice at them and be aware of how well they are coping – just like teaching (substantive) concepts, except they are the same concepts (of evidence) every time, but in different situations. And just like (substantive) concepts, some kids don't get them all. But more kids can get more of these substantive concepts than they can of knowledge and what's more – it applies to other places in their lives where they think. So you're going to get a developing 'thinking method' going as a framework in which to explore the world, and if necessary you can 'test out' the knowledge you are learning. Seeing whether you really understand.

You've got to get them going, and then stop them in their tracks and make them think about what they're doing. Shock them into believing in their own reasoning powers. That there's no right and wrong except what they decide based on the evidence in front of them. And you've got to use strategies that show some of them are thinking like this – use the differences in investigations that arise to learn from each other. Point out that it is significant when someone does use their reasoning powers successfully.

All a scheme of work can do is:

- put in investigations regularly – content chosen normally (based in traditional topic areas).
- think about investigations in terms of procedural complexity – don't make them too hard to start with, then they can get harder. Context varying; sometimes scientific. In other words, build in progression.
- allow opportunities in between investigations for practising procedural understanding (follow-up activities). Just have as many ways as possible for getting them in those situations where they have to think. So – giving them a graph to draw and interpret, getting information from tables, brainstorming. We're trying to find more and better ways. Ways to get them to think about these things. You have to keep varying the approach or they get bored and won't think.
- now the flexibility must come in, as with any scheme of work. What do the kids do in an investigation? Once you know this, you can then focus on the weaknesses and strengths of (their understanding of) concepts of evidence in discussion. Do they (strengths and weaknesses) match the ones planned for in the scheme of work? And then whether the kids are strong in that area, or weak, there is either a reinforcing aspect or a teaching aspect.

There can be no linear formula; it is the building of a round picture where all the aspects interlink gradually and individually and differently in different situations.

1 Open investigation

The topic of friction is introduced with an open investigation:

What affects the slippiness of training shoes?

It is set in context orally perhaps in the gym, or outside if it happens to be winter and icy underfoot. There is no specific teaching focus to the task: the aim is to open up the topic of friction and allow children's ideas to emerge. It may transpire that most children understand that, for instance, weight and area have an effect. But it could reveal misconceptions about force or problems associated with its measurement. In any event, it sets the scene for what is to follow. The understanding revealed in this first investigation may mean that some of the following parts can be omitted. Alternatively, if unexpected gaps in understanding are revealed, some additions may need to be made.

2 Choosing and using forcemeters

The appropriate skill of measuring force is introduced using a skills exercise where pupils are asked to measure different things such as opening a drawer, a door, etc. Pupils are allowed access to a range of forcemeters so that they have to decide which is the most appropriate for the task they have selected.

3 The concept of friction

To extend pupils' ideas which the teacher had begun to elicit in the training shoe exercise, the question 'What is friction?' can be used as the topic for a teacher-led discussion of friction and its causes and effects.

4 Illustrating the concept and its measurement

Here a demonstration using blocks with different surfaces can be used to illustrate the idea that friction depends on weight and surface. Alternatively, a tightly controlled worksheet-driven session could be used.

5 A targeted investigation which uses these ideas

To put the investigation into a context, a video on the theme of the making of the pyramids can be used as an introduction. Pupils are then asked:

> What do you think might affect how difficult it would be to pull a brick up a slope?
>
> (One of the ideas was probably the angle of the slope)
>
> Do an investigation to:
>
> Find out how the angle of the slope affects how easy it is to pull a brick up.
>
> When you have finished, your teacher will ask you to work out the best slope for somebody who can only pull with a certain force. So you will need to collect data that will allow you to do this.

This investigation can be presented in a variety of other ways, some of which can be used as supplementary or alternative investigations for the more able pupils. Or, lest boredom set in, one of them could be the subject of a teacher-led demonstration with the pupils directing operations.

> Another way of moving the stones is to use a block and tackle. Make one using two pulley blocks. Find out what difference the block and tackle makes.
>
> The smoothness of the surface makes a lot of difference. If you were a pyramid builder would it be better to spend time making a very smooth slope or use the time to make a long shallow slope?

6 Follow-up exercises (used at various points in the sequence as appropriate)

The investigation will have revealed strengths and weaknesses in pupils' procedural understanding. Exercises such as those in Chapter 6 can be used here to target particular concepts of evidence. If some groups find interpreting data difficult, for example, they could be given other groups' data to practise interpretation. If pupils are unsure of the use of tables, they could be given a worksheet on how tables can be used to structure design and data collection.

Some of these exercises may be needed by most pupils, so that it may be useful to organise a class exercise and/or discussion. Alternatively, if only a few pupils are weak in a particular area, then the exercise can be given for homework for reinforcement.

After three years of work in this area, the message is that schemes of work must be comprised of a series of signposts – key learning outcomes. Navigation between these signposts must be at the discretion of the teacher, and in response to all the vagaries of real-life teaching. But it needs a resource of investigations of various types, and follow-up work, and strategies for teaching and learning to hand. Having said that, schemes of work have to start somewhere. The following is an example of a teaching sequence that could be *developed* into a scheme of work. The substantive concept we have chosen is friction, on no better grounds than that all of the activities have been tested in the classroom at one time or another.

The scheme of work can then continue in a similar vein, interspersing investigations in order to use substantive concepts which have already been introduced and to develop procedural understanding. Table 7.1 summarises the purposes of each lesson.

It is from such a table that we can begin the task of creating schemes of work. All too often a scheme of work is little more than sets of lesson notes. What we should be aiming for is a route map through the learning outcomes – the things that we hope pupils will understand afterwards that they didn't before. Once the learning outcomes are identified, the activities that are best suited to those outcomes can be designed.

Table 7.2 is an edited version of part of one such scheme of work. The start of the first year (pupils aged 11 in a comprehensive school) consisted of a three-week module called 'Be scientific', followed by a longer module introducing materials in a topic called 'Our earth'.

Progression

Looking back over a pupil's work, it should be possible to see that there has been progression on a variety of fronts. The example on p. 102 is by Michelle, an average year 7 (12-year-old) pupil in a comprehensive school in the North-East. We have chosen it from many examples because it is not untypical of the way pupils learn, progressing and then regressing. What follows is a summary of Michelle's progression in procedural understanding beginning with the work in the scheme outlined on p. 102.

Table 7.1 Beginning a scheme of work on friction

The lesson/activity	Principal learning outcome	Conceptual understanding	Procedural understanding
Open investigation	Diagnostic assessment of conceptual understanding	√	
Choosing and using forcemeters	Skill and concept of evidence (choice of instrument)		√
The concept of friction	To reinforce the concept of friction by relating it to familiar situations	√	
Illustrating the concept and its measurement	To introduce and/or develop the idea of measuring friction as a force	√	
A targeted investigation which *uses* these ideas	Applying the concept of force and assessing procedural understanding	√	√
Follow-up exercises	Reinforcing particular concepts of evidence		√

Table 7.2 Elements of a scheme of work

Be scientific	Learning outcome	Suggested activities
General introduction to lab safety	Key danger points in a laboratory	Discussion centred on pictures of dangerous lab situations, poster session. Using a Bunsen burner
Heating things safely and measuring temperature	Understanding tables and interpreting data	Basic skill activity on thermometers
		Investigation into insulating materials to keep hot potato hot
Heat transfer via conduction	Insulators and conductors of heat	Discussion plus demonstration or class experiment on conduction
Insulators	Applying understanding about tables and checking on the notion of a fair test	Investigation into the best type of material for a disposable hot drinks cup
Follow-up work	The idea of variables, identifying variables (as independent and so on), recording the data and their interpretation, and the link between a fair test and the validity of the data	Discussion of class results on the drinks cup investigation. Follow-up work on interpreting other people's data

In the first investigation, which involved different materials wrapped around hot potatoes, her record consisted of:

> Change: material
> Keep the same: size/type of potato, time
> Results: 46°C before, 46°C after.

The class then pooled their results and one of the outcomes was a table on the board which was transcribed into their books. In a second, related, investigation concerning the type of cup and its ability to keep drinks warm, there was some degree of progress, but in the idea of a fair test rather than in tables!

> Timed it for 5 minutes and it dropped 8°C. Another one (the polystyrene cup) dropped 7°C. This means that the polystyrene cup is the best insulator. But we did not measure how much water we put in each. I think we could of [sic] had a more accurate answer.

Later, in the second module on 'materials', there followed an exercise on interpretation of graphs. Michelle began to make progress in understanding bar charts here and then moved into an investigation – to find out which paper is best to use for holding chips? Her results table was a considerable improvement:

	Recycled paper	Grease proof paper	New improved paper
First trial	500 g	300 g	400 g
Second trial	400 g	200 g	500 g
Third trial	400 g	200 g	500 g

Her notebook also showed evidence of understanding fair tests and repeats. Two further investigations interspersed within the module were carried out reasonably well including tables, bar charts and fair tests. The final investigation in the module concerned the bounciness of squash balls – how does the bounciness depend on temperature? This is a type 2 investigation with a continuous independent variable. All the others had been type 1. And at this point Michelle goes to pieces:

We did our test and dropped the ball from 2 m.
We did this three times.
Then we wrote our results table.
My results:
The first trial was 96 cm.
The second trial was 90 cm.
The third trial was 96 cm.
The average was 94 cm.

She drew a bar chart of these four values. Her conclusion was: 'The pattern in my graph goes up and down.'

Like the ball. Michelle was completely thrown by the continuous variable issue to such an extent that she seems to have fallen back on the last thing she got a positive comment on, the averaging of three results. This regression happens often. The only remedy is repetition, so that the notion of understanding, evidenced in the early investigations, is transformed into the ability to *apply* in novel situations.

Some practical considerations

A note on introducing the language of investigations

It is not uncommon when discussing investigations with pupils, for them to express a sense of uncertainty as to what it is they have learned. With other practical work such as an experiment called 'Hooke's Law', they know that that is what they are supposed to have learned. Furthermore, they can refer to the activity in their books and during revision as the 'Hooke's Law' experiment, even if they don't fully understand it.

For example, the extent to which the language of the concepts of evidence we have proposed should be part of the language of teaching is not at all

clear. It is certainly true that before pupils can begin investigations, they need to understand *some* of the basic language which is associated with them. The question is: Which ideas need to have their own language and what is that language to be? Terms such as 'variable' and 'control' can present difficulty for some pupils. Various alternative phraseologies have been suggested to try to overcome the problem, some of which are shown in Table 7.3.

There is an argument for the 'thing to change' approach to do with the accessibility of the language. But there is a counter-argument which says that the search for simple words can lead to confusion and that it is better to deal with the language head-on using the 'correct' terms from the word go. The first three activities in the CASE project adopt this approach by introducing the terms input and outcome variables. The ground rules in terms of language are carefully established and then used consistently throughout the remaining activities.

In the example overleaf, taken from the NCC research, we see that Jonathan, when prompted to write what he would change, says that he would 'change nothing', whereas in the sense that the prompt was intended, he did indeed change the independent variable. What he was referring to, we may surmise, is that he controlled the other appropriate variables and did a 'fair test'.

The word 'control' in relation to variables can also create difficulties because of its confusion with the biological meaning of 'control'. In the latter, the control refers to the condition of no treatment (e.g. the effect of no fertiliser on growth), which in investigations equates with a zero value of the independent variable. This is quite different from the meaning of control variables. A further difficulty arises with categoric variables. The term

Table 7.3 Alternative ways of describing variables

The independent variable	*The dependent variable*	*The variables to be controlled*
The 'thing' to change (systematically)	The 'thing' to measure (for each value of the independent variable)	The 'things' to keep the same to make the test fair
The input variable	The outcome variable	

> **Jonathan (year 7, aged 11)**
>
> Find out how the distance moved by the model depends on the amount the elastic band is stretched.

The bigger the elastic band stretched the farther it will go.

We are going to change nothing.

The things we will measure are the farther the tub gone and how fare we pull the elastic band back.

'variables' is sometimes associated only with numerical quantities, so that the idea that the type of insulating material can also be a variable (a categoric variable) with 'values' such as polystyrene or cloth, needs careful introduction.

The 'fair test', too, has presented difficulty, particularly in primary science. There is some anecdotal evidence to show that pupils see a fair test as being concerned with keeping everything in sight the same because the very name 'fair' suggests that not to do that is somehow unfair. To other children, the notion of a fair test is akin to a handicap in horse racing. If the horse is fast, it should carry extra weight to slow it down. 'Fairness' in science means something quite different from 'fairness' in a horse race or a playground brawl.

The above examples show the importance of establishing the ground rules in language early on to avoid misunderstandings and confusion. It is also necessary to reinforce these terms by their consistent use in all experimental work, whichever set of terms is selected. Some concepts are closely associated, so that they are likely to be taught together. For example, the concept of the pattern in line graphs cannot be understood without some understanding of range and interval. Whether other terms such as relative scale, validity and so on need to be used, and if so when they should be introduced, needs further classroom-based research.

Organising investigations in the science laboratory

The organisation of the working groups within the class depends to some extent on the nature of the problem to be investigated and its degree of openness. Where the problem is closely defined, the whole class will usually carry out the same investigation, each group deciding on its own methodology. In terms of preparation and control, many teachers will find this is the most straightforward arrangement. More open problems may lead to different investigations, in the same context, being carried out within the same class, which will clearly require a wider range of equipment. An example of this situation is when the teacher begins the lesson by raising questions about a concept such as friction (as in the sample scheme of work on p. 100) and asks the pupils to identify factors which could affect the slippiness of a training shoe. Variables such as the type or area of the sole, the weight of the person wearing the shoe, the pattern of the tread and so on, can all be developed into investigations by different groups. Jones *et al.* (1992) provide some useful case studies of ways of engaging pupils through the use of brainstorming techniques or stimulus activities or events.

A further possibility is to have apparently unrelated investigations being done simultaneously where a particular concept of evidence is the common factor. Hence the lesson might focus on data interpretation or the significance of repeated readings. Having children present their data to the rest of the class who have not done the same task, can be a very useful exercise which can promote 'bridging' of procedural understanding (cf. CASE, Chapter 2). Clearly, there are problems of organisation in this approach in that much apparatus is necessary, but a further advantage in this approach is that it can emphasise to pupils that acquiring procedural understanding is a significant part of science.

Prompt sheets

Various ways can be used to offer guidance to the pupils as to what is expected of them. The prompt

Your report
Make sure you think about what you were trying to find out.
Did you include:
what you were trying to find out?
what you altered?
what you measured?
how you made your investigation a fair test?
how many measurements you made?
what instruments you used to make your measurements?
how accurate your measurements were (e.g. to the nearest millimetre)?
a result table?
a graph or a description of the pattern in words?
what you found out?
why your results could be believed by other people?
a conclusion which matched your results?
an explanation of your results using scientific ideas?

Fig. 7.1 A prompt sheet (Gott *et al.*, 1992)

sheet shown in Fig. 7.1 is one possibility. The prompt sheet can also serve as a reminder to the teacher to emphasise to pupils the significance of their record as a scientific report for others who may not have done the activity. It is therefore important that the validity and reliability of their evidence is clear in their write-ups. Prompt sheets can be adapted to the needs of the children (e.g. according to age) and the focus of the lesson.

The danger of such prompt sheets is that they become much like the rigid format of the past where each experiment had set headings such as title, apparatus, method, results and conclusions. Nevertheless, the pros probably outweigh the cons in that they can be used to establish and reinforce learning objectives. They also familiarise the pupils with the language used to describe learning objectives which is also the language of assessment. It is also possible to use a variety of styles for different tasks and year groups.

The role of the teacher in the investigation

Skilful and appropriate questioning is probably the most important role for the teacher in investi-

gations. There has been a tendency to see investigations as a 'do-it-yourself' exercise for pupils with minimal or no teacher intervention. Indeed, the swing away from didactic to child-centred teaching may have further reinforced the idea that intervention is a 'bad thing'. Investigations are indeed about empowering children to apply knowledge, but it is essential that the teacher acts as a skilful mediator in the process. Indeed, Foulds *et al.* (1992) suggest that investigations require *greater interaction*. The teacher has above all to be flexible in meeting the needs of individual pupils. Revell (1993) suggests planning 'enabling questions' before the lesson. These are questions that 'the teacher plans to ask in order to advance children's learning or reveal achievement of a learning objective'. Some examples of enabling questions are shown in Table 7.4.

Foulds *et al.* (1992) point to the critical role of the timing of the intervention here:

[The teacher] must recognise when to intervene, and also when it is more appropriate not to intervene. Intervention too early means that pupils will be unable to recognise the relevance of the

Table: 7.4 Examples from an enabling question planner (Revell, 1993)

Learning objectives	Enabling questions
Interpret	What do your results mean?
	Was your prediction right?
	Is there a mathematical pattern in your results?
Communicate	Which is the best way to tell others what you did and what you found out?
	Do your results go best in a table/ chart /graph?
Evaluate	What do your results mean?
	What else could your results mean?
	How can you tell that is what your results really mean?

intervening discussion and suggestions – the intervention may be seen as direction, rather than support, removing ownership from the pupil.

As the pupils collect data, they should be encouraged by the teacher to reflect on their meaning so that ongoing modifications can be made to the investigation:

> 'do you think this (the dependent variable) will double if that (the independent variable) is doubled?' can encourage reflection on the number, range and value of the data being collected, and help pupils extend the scope of their findings.
>
> (Foulds *et al.*, 1992).

Foulds *et al.* (1992) suggest that the teacher may take on a variety of other less obvious roles throughout the investigation such as: manager in terms of controlling behaviour, motivator and provider of encouragement thus empowering the less confident pupils to proceed with their own strategy.

Reporting-back session

After the practical part of the investigation is over, the discussion which follows and centres on groups reporting-back is vital. The importance of this stage of the investigation is frequently underestimated and on occasion bypassed altogether (admittedly sometimes because of the pressure of time). The reporting-back session has to be carefully handled so that its learning outcomes are achieved. It is at this point that most concepts of evidence take on their full impact because pupils now have to use their evidence to support their conclusions. The notion of audience discussed in Chapter 2 is particularly relevant here in encouraging pupils to provide valid and reliable evidence to support a conclusion.

Jones *et al.* (1992) suggest that the reporting stage be followed by a 'consolidation' stage where the pupils are encouraged to use the information gained to further their knowledge and understanding. This kind of reflective discussion, where the learning outcomes of the groups in the class are shared, can be very useful.

A note on resources and safety

Resources are a particular problem in investigative work. A wide range of instruments must be made available, e.g. an adequate number of forcemeters with different scales. If only the basic equipment for the investigation is displayed, then the element of choosing the most appropriate instrument is lost. While this might appear to be unrealistic in times of economic restraint, the equipment for investigations is in the main relatively basic, the more complex and specialised equipment being only necessary at the higher levels.

The related issue of accessibility to equipment is also important, enabling pupils to select easily from a central store or trolley. Where it is feasible, a set of storage trays which are labelled with the name of the investigation and which contain those resources which are particular to it (bags of different types of sugar, for instance) can be set up. A separate rack of labelled trays can be kept for measuring equipment. For instance, a tray labelled *measuring forces* would contain a range of appropriate instruments.

Revell (1993) points out that an understanding of safety is part of science education, so that the children should be involved in assessing the risk of the investigation. Among other helpful practical strategies for overcoming the problem, Revell *et al.* suggest using a colour code to indicate the degree of risk associated with an activity:

- red activities: greater risk and a lot of supervision required
- amber activities: medium risk, some supervision required
- green activities: low risk with little direct supervision necessary.

The authors suggest that the class can then be organised so that, for instance, only one red activity is going on, amber activities are positioned near the teacher and the rest of the class are engaged in green or non-practical activities.

Summary

Schemes of work are an essential element of a teacher's armoury. In the context of procedural understanding, a scheme of work has to cope with the idea that the concepts of evidence, which are relatively few in number compared to substantive concepts, reappear in many contexts. The task of incorporating progression into the scheme, alongside progression in substantive concepts, is not easy. The best that can be done is to highlight the signposts – the concepts of evidence that constitute the learning outcomes – that define progression and then work in targeted investigations and follow-up work where it is most sensible to do so. And be ready for pupils who go backwards in their use of tables and fair tests and so on when they hit a new idea like continuous variables. Then those ideas have to be recycled to show pupils that they still apply.

Another part of the armoury is a set of resources such as prompt sheets and pupil self-assessment records (see the next chapter). These in turn rely on an agreed language to describe such things as categoric or independent variables. We have made a few tentative suggestions in this regard, but the issue is far from resolved due mainly to the fact that investigative work has only just started to become the focus for development in Key Stage 4, where it becomes far more important as pupils need a common language to describe their understandings.

And yet another weapon must be the quality of teacher intervention in the classroom. There is a tendency to regard investigative work as being the same as the discovery learning of the 1960s. From this stance, the received wisdom would have been to allow pupils to discover things for themselves with little if any intervention by the teacher. In fact, teacher intervention, and indeed straightforward teaching, is an absolutely essential part of investigative work. Pupils do need to try things out, but then they need to be brought to see that there are better ways of doing things; encouraged and led and, if necessary, driven to improve their understanding.

References

Foulds, K., Gott, R. and Feasey, R. (1992). *Investigative Work in Science.* Durham, University of Durham.

Gott, R., Costello, H. and Foulds, K. (1992). Materials to support the assessment of Sc1. Draft document, Durham University.

Jones, A.T., Simon, S.A., Black, P.J., Fairbrother, R.W. and Watson, J.R. (1992). *Open Work in Science: Development of Investigations in Schools.* Hatfield, Association for Science Education.

Revell, M. (ed.) (1993). *The Sc1 Book of Investigations, 5–16.* Northamptonshire Inspection and Advisory Service. Northampton, Northamptonshire County Council.

CHAPTER 8

Assessment

Assessment can refer to the assessment of the pupil's potential ability or it can refer to attainment. It is the second of these, attainment, which will primarily concern us here. While attainment depends on underlying ability, it also depends on other factors such as motivation and teaching.

The purpose of the assessment of a pupil's attainment might be:

- *formative:* aimed at deciding what the next step in a curriculum plan or the teacher's scheme of work should be for that individual or group; or
- *diagnostic:* aimed at determining lack of understanding or any weak points, for any individual or group, so that remedial action can be taken; or
- *summative:* aimed at providing a measure of the level of attainment which pupils have achieved. This measure, grade or mark may be required for pupils to progress to the next stage of their education or to other institutions in the education system.

Formative and diagnostic assessments aim to assess in a detailed and thorough way the breadth and depth of the pupils' knowledge of a particular subject area. Summative assessment, on the other hand, *samples* knowledge and understanding in that only some parts of the subject area will be selected for testing. All of these types of assessment are assessments of, and for the benefit of, the individual.

In recent years, the APU, NAEP (National Assessment of Educational Progress) in the USA and other such organisations have organised assessments which are in reality evaluations of the curriculum and the school system rather than of the individual. These assessments are, of course, carried out through the testing of individual pupils but in other regards this form of assessment can be very different. There is, for instance, no need to assess all pupils; a random sample is adequate provided the sampling frame takes into account the smallest unit of interest to policy makers. That unit of interest could be, for example, a school, a local education authority or a region, or it may be a particular group of pupils, such as those of low ability, or boys. There is no need to insist that all pupils do the same 'test' provided the groups are matched. So one group could do a practical investigation, while another matched group might do a different one, or a related skills circus.

The point we are making is that it is essential to be clear about the purpose and nature of the assessment because this will determine not so much the test items themselves, but the structure and organisation of the testing and the way the resulting scores are recorded, aggregated and used.

This chapter will deal with a variety of techniques of assessment linked to the type of quantitative investigations used in the NCC research. The ideas discussed here are not intended to be a complete catalogue for assessment. Rather, they are a menu from which appropriate activities can be chosen, augmented and refined for whichever of the above purposes is under consideration. We shall consider first what it is we are trying to assess in investigations and then move on to explore ways of carrying out the assessment.

What is to be assessed?

In the last chapter, we noted that while pupils apply their conceptual understanding at particular points in the investigation, facts and concepts are, arguably, more efficiently taught, and likewise assessed, by means of more traditional methods. Investigations can and do allow opportunities for children to demonstrate their understanding of science concepts; we have argued throughout this book that investigative work involves both conceptual and procedural understanding. But using investigations to assess conceptual understanding would be to select the wrong tool for the job. What can be noted, in passing, is that much diagnostic information about pupils' understandings does emerge from the way they tackle an investigation. We quoted examples in Chapter 7 which show how implicit understandings can surface from investigations; insights such as the idea that heat can be packed into a hard-boiled egg, which

may be unobtainable from more traditional testing methods.

The thrust of our argument has been that investigations are a unique opportunity in practical science to teach procedural understanding and that this understanding has its own 'content', of skills and concepts of evidence which have to be *taught*. It follows that assessment must be based around this selfsame content. So we cannot begin with the assessment of *investigations* as if that were an end in itself. Rather, we must begin with the things that pupils should 'know, understand and be able to do' in the area of procedural understanding. This distinction is an important one in that it now allows us to see investigations as *one* form of assessment among many. Before we move on to look at this, it may be useful to set traditional forms of examining within this view of procedural understanding.

Traditional assessment

Examining practical work

When we look at most examination syllabuses for science, the influence of Bloom's taxonomy can be seen clearly. The Northern Examining Association's

Table 8.1 The specific assessment objectives for 'Experimental work' (NEA, 1992, 1993) and their main emphases

The examination will test:	Comment
1 Experimental work Candidates should be able to: 1 follow instructions for practical work; 2 select appropriate apparatus; 3 handle and manipulate chemical apparatus and material…safely; 4 make accurate observations and measurements, being aware of the possible sources of error; 5 record accurately and clearly the results of experiments; 6 draw conclusions and make generalisations from experiments; 7 plan and organise experimental investigations to test hypotheses.	If the assessment is made of each point separately, the emphasis is likely to be very firmly on skills and, to a lesser extent, isolated concepts of evidence. The context may be a skills circus or one based in illustrative practicals where pupils are asked to draw conclusions, having carried out a recipe type activity. Only point 7 will result in pupils having to apply and synthesise skills and concepts of evidence. If, on the other hand, the assessment is made in the context of investigative work, which is quite possible although unusual, most of the points will be interlinked and shift the emphasis somewhat more towards concepts of evidence. What is clear, however, is that only some concepts of evidence are addressed explicitly.

(NEA) syllabus for the 1992 and 1993 examinations in chemistry, for example, has four assessment objectives, three of which are principally concerned with substantive concepts (2, 3 and 4):

1 Experimental work
2 Knowledge and recall
3 Understanding
4 Application, analysis, synthesis and evaluation

It is interesting to note here how experimental work has been detached from the other three objectives as if it were a separate entity. We can look more closely at this breakdown in the light of our definition of procedural understanding. Table 8.1 shows how the NEA defines 'Experimental work' and how it might address aspects of procedural understanding.

Non-practical examining

A modular science scheme by the NEA included an assessment of data interpretation (for example, Scheme A – Single Award /First Award module, 1989). These written papers were innovative in the sense that the pupils were not required to bring any particular science knowledge to the exam. Instead,

they were given accessible concepts and contexts in which to show their understanding of data interpretation. An example is given in Table 8.2.

The examples cited demonstrate how different examination boards and schemes met the National Criteria for Science which were developed in the 1980s prior to the introduction of the National Curriculum. What was emerging, tentatively and rather patchily, was a more differentiated form of assessment which was creating, and therefore enhancing, the importance of what we have called skills and concepts of evidence in more open-ended types of practical work. The framework was not particularly well-articulated, nor were terms particularly well-defined, but the seeds had been sown. We shall see in the next chapter how these seeds were transplanted into the National Curriculum.

Assessing procedural understanding

We have already suggested that the procedural taxonomy, linked to a definition of skills and concepts of evidence, allows for a more focused approach in the teaching of investigative work. Clearly, those same ideas, constituting as they do

Table 8.2 Example of an examination question on data interpretation: NEA Science (Modular) Paper 1, Scheme A – Single Award/First Award 1989

A small house was built about 50 years ago. It costs £500 a year to heat the house.

The table below shows how much money could be saved by improving the house in various ways.

Improvement	Cost	Saving on fuel each year	Time taken to pay for improvement
Insulating spaces between walls	£300	£60	5 years
Insulating loft	£300	£100	
Draught proofing doors and windows	£25	£50	
Double glazing	£1500	£50	

(a) Which improvement saves most money on fuel each year?

(b) Complete the last column in the table above.

(c) From the information given in the table, suggest which improvement should be made *first*.

Give a reason for your answer.

a 'content' for procedural understanding, can act as a set of assessment objectives. For completeness, we reproduce the taxonomy here:

Procedural taxonomy

- Knowledge and recall of skills
- Understanding of concepts of evidence
- Application of concepts of evidence
- Synthesis of concepts of evidence

Assessments can be produced for each of the elements of the taxonomy, which we shall consider in turn.

Assessing the recall and use of skills

The definition of skills we have adopted is to some extent experience-dependent. So the first task in assessing skills is to decide what activities are appropriate for the age range, ability and background of the pupils. Having done that, a choice must be made as to whether the assessment is to be embedded in an illustrative experiment or an investigation. We shall deal first with the assessment of the skill in isolation. The assessment task then must clearly focus on the appropriate skill(s)

Table 8.3 A measuring skills exercise (from Gott *et al.*, 1988).

Using instruments

In front of you are a number of measuring instruments which you will need to use to answer these questions. Do not forget to say what UNITS you are using.

What is the temperature of this laboratory?

The temperature is ....

How long does it take for the ball bearing to roll down the track?

The time is ....

How heavy is the ball bearing you have just used?

The mass is ....

---

with as little distraction as possible. An example of a circus practical where several measurement skills are tested is given in Table 8.3.

The pupils are given one of each type of measuring instrument – a suitable thermometer, stopwatch and scales so that the choice is one of selecting the thermometer to measure temperature rather than of choosing one of several thermometers. The assessment is, therefore, primarily of skills and only to a limited extent of concepts of evidence (pupils might, for instance, show understanding of appropriate accuracy and repeatability). Other examples suitable for assessment purposes can be found in a number of published texts (e.g. Coles *et al.*, 1988, 1989; Gott *et al.*, 1991).

We would argue that such assessment should be used for diagnostic purposes since skill deficits may have unlooked-for, and possibly unrecognised, consequences for more complex assessments. For instance, an assessment in which pupils are required to weigh an item, may give quite the wrong impression of the pupil's attainment if he or she avoids weighing simply because of ignorance as to how to use the scales. Similarly, Strang (1990), reporting the work of the APU, showed how pupils often read individual divisions on a particular scale incorrectly so that all subsequent readings are inaccurate.

Skills assessment, therefore, can be diagnostic in that common errors can be spotted. It may also be used for summative assessment, such as in the circus practical (Table 8.3) where a 'mark scheme' can be implemented by simply counting the number of skills a pupil can accomplish successfully.

Such marking can be applied, in theory, to assessing the same skill in the context of an illustrative or investigative task. The danger of so doing is that this element of the assessment, because it is relatively easy to carry out, takes over from the more important assessment of understanding and application which is more time-consuming and requires judgement rather than relying mechanistically on 'bits' of evidence. Diagnostic assessment of skills at an early stage is nevertheless essential if basic errors in, for example, using equipment, are to be avoided.

Assessing the understanding and application of individual concepts of evidence in short assessment tasks

We argued in the last chapter that the teaching of some concepts of evidence in isolation is just not possible because the ideas are so enmeshed in the whole investigation that any attempt to isolate them ends up with an unwieldy and, probably, invalid activity. Nevertheless, some concepts of evidence can be isolated. Examples of those associated with the concepts of fair testing, choice of instrument, data handling and interpretation were given in the last chapter. These exercises can, of course, be used for summative, formative or diagnostic assessment.

Assessing the synthesis of concepts of evidence

Putting together ideas about how evidence can be generated, interpreted and evaluated can, in theory, be assessed using a variety of activities. Investigations are, we would argue, the principal type of practical science activity in which pupils are given the opportunity to synthesise skills and concepts of evidence into an overall strategy. We intend to discuss only the sorts of investigation described in earlier chapters because those are the only ones for which data on pupil performance are available in a form appropriate to the discussion.

Using investigations for assessment purposes

Choosing the investigation

In Chapter 6, we discussed the issue of progression in investigative work and its link to the complexity and sophistication of the data in the light of the research evidence presented in Chapters 4 and 5. The arguments raised there are relevant to the choice of task, since it is important to achieve some sort of match between task type and structure and the attainment of any individual pupil or group. The choice of an investigation also requires a not inconsiderable degree of experience to allow for anticipation of the wide range of ideas that pupils come up with.

The research evidence, however, points to some key factors which help to govern the choice of investigations:

Substantive concepts

In Chapter 4, we saw the strong but sometimes unexpected effect that concepts have on performance. In terms of assessing procedural understanding, it follows that it is essential to use *several different* concept areas that are at a level well within the grasp of the pupils. If the concepts are too hard or unfamiliar, their effect can be to block the pupils at an early stage of the investigation. Several tasks allow for the fact that pupils find some tasks easier, or more motivating, or both, and perform better.

The context

The research evidence shows that, if the context is 'everyday', then children can regress in their performance. For assessment purposes, it might therefore be tempting to use only scientific contexts. Our suggestion is that if everyday contexts are used regularly in the normal teaching situation interspersed with scientific contexts, then children will begin to relate science to everyday situations and perform as well in either context.

Procedural complexity

Differentiation in assessment can be by outcome or by task. Differentiation by outcome relies on the use of a task which allows all pupils to make progress, but encourages the more able to carry out a more sophisticated investigation. By definition almost, the task will need to be set in a more open form, which can cause problems as pupils opting for the easy life carry out an investigation well below their capacity. For instance, in the investigation 'Which is the best fuel?', able pupils may opt to design an investigation where they interpret the dependent variable as 'the smokiest' and then proceed to measure qualitatively. They may well be capable of carrying out highly competent work of the sort exemplified at the end of the last chapter.

Alternatively, as we saw in the last chapter in the case of the apple juice task, investigations can be relatively easily manipulated in terms of procedural complexity on the basis of variable structure within one context. Thus, in a mixed-ability class, assessment can be carried out by using a series of slightly different investigations of varying complexity appropriate to the ability of the pupils. Even within a more targeted task, there is an element of differentiation by outcome which will allow pupils who fail to rise to the challenge to carry out a lower-level investigation.

Openness

The effect of the openness of the task definition was to depress performance because children tended to opt for 'easier' investigations and regress to qualitative comparisons, although encouragement from the teacher or prompt sheets may help here.

It is clear that from the point of view of assessment of procedural understanding, the favourite, in terms of manageability, is an investigation which is defined relatively tightly but which is then quite open in terms of method and solution. This will allow for a degree of control over predictions while retaining the key elements of allowing pupils to select their own method and put together their own solution.

The importance of question wording

The wording or language of the task is also important. Obviously, the language must be at a level easily understandable by the pupils, particularly in an assessment situation. There is no reason, of course, why a written form of the task should not be supplemented by an oral introduction from the teacher.

The wording is also important in determining the choice of design. For example in the investigation 'Does the temperature of the water affect how quickly the sugar dissolves?', it could be argued that testing hot and cold water is sufficient to answer the question. Changing the wording to 'How does the temperature of the water affect the time the sugar takes to dissolve?' might convey to

the expert the idea that a relationship is looked for, but it is a very subtle point for pupils which may easily be missed. Various techniques can be used to encourage pupils to explore relationships more fully. An example for younger secondary pupils is given in Fig. 8.1. The competition at the end serves to focus the pupils' attention on the need for some method of prediction, based on the relationship between the variables, which will show how far the bottle will go. A line graph is just such a predictor.

The last point concerning wording is to do with the pupil's written account. We will see in the next section that these accounts are valuable pieces of evidence, so we should endeavour to make them as complete as possible. Pupils can be encouraged to give fuller accounts by giving them a target audience to write for, such as a relative, or a friend in a different class, or the environmental health inspector. Occasionally, this technique can backfire unexpectedly with pupils writing in unscientific terms; they need constantly to be reminded that they are to present *scientific* evidence which will convince someone else.

Class 3 were running a Cola bar in aid of a local charity. They set up a catapult to shoot Cola bottles down the bar to the customer.

This is the question you have to find an answer to:

How does the distance the bottle travels depend on how far the elastic is pulled back?

When you have finished, your teacher will tell you where the first customer will sit.
You have to be able to shoot the Cola bottle straight to them. No trial runs!
Prizes for the nearest.

Fig. 8.1 The Cola bottle investigation (Gott, 1993)

In summary, then, we suggest that the following be considered as criteria for selecting investigations for assessment purposes:

- three or four tasks in different concept areas which have been taught and are, in general, reasonably well understood by the pupils;
- set in a mix of everyday and scientific contexts;
- differentiated by task, with some pupils being asked to carry out type 1 investigations, others type 2 and so on;
- with a well-defined question but choice of method and solution;
- an oral introduction to set the scene and to supplement the written task;
- having a clearly stated purpose;
- a target audience for the pupils' reports which encourages as complete a description as possible;
- access to a wide range of appropriate resources where possible so that ideally pupils will be able to select an appropriate instrument;
- accompanied by constant, but neutral, encouragement from the teacher.

Having selected the investigations, the next issue concerns the collection of evidence on which to base the assessment. It is all too easy for the session to become dominated by checklists to the exclusion of judgement. It is to the management of the assessment session that we must now turn.

Collecting evidence for assessment

The assessment of investigations can be done through a combination of observation of the pupils 'in action' by the teacher, children's written accounts and, if possible, through questioning of pupils. In addition, children's self-assessment records can be used to inform the overall assessment. There is also the pragmatic issue of assessing children while they are working in groups.

Group work

While tradition dictates that pupils should be assessed individually in exam conditions (for summative reporting at any rate), the realities of practical work in the classroom are likely to make

such an approach unreasonably time-consuming and disruptive. Pupils working in a group inevitably work differently from any one of them alone, that is the nature of communal effort. But when pupils are asked to write up their work individually, their understanding or lack of it can show up starkly. Since we are assessing the *understanding* of concepts of evidence, then these written reports are vital. That is not to say that other forms of assessment are not necessary. We shall see in the following sections how different assessment methods can all contribute to an overview of pupil performance. Experience shows that professional judgement over a series of tasks will allow for assessment of an individual in the context of group work. What cannot be said as yet is the degree to which working in a group influences an individual's *understanding* of the task.

Observation

The observation of practical work by the teacher can be carried out in two ways. The teacher can simply watch groups of pupils and come to a judgement. Or, the teacher can use a standardised checklist in an attempt to gain objectivity. Checklists, or the 'ticky box' approach as one teacher in a local school calls it, can be cumbersome and are an anathema to many professional teachers. They also run the risk of teachers not seeing the wood for the trees: because they are focusing on the detail, they may lose sight of the quality of the investigation as a whole.

We will declare an interest here on behalf of the judges rather than the accountants. We believe that the 'stand back' judgement is a better reflection of the synthesis which we believe to be the key to investigative work. Our arguments in this regard are not based on any reliable empirical evidence but on experience of teachers engaged in the task.

But there is a proviso. We believe that a mental checklist *is* needed to inform that judgement. Experience suggests that, in practice, it might well be necessary to use the checklist approach, at least initially, until it becomes an automatic one which will inform, but not be the only component of, the overall judgement. The checklist is also a means of assessing the understanding and application of individual, or a particular subset of, concepts of evidence such as those associated with data handling or design.

The complex checklists used by the APU and by the NCC project were designed for research purposes and so are not necessarily useful in situations where teacher judgement is, quite rightly, an important element. To provide evidence about procedural understanding and to inform the judgement which has to be made against the criteria, we suggest that a much shorter checklist based on skills and concepts of evidence should be used and, further, that the checklist should be general rather than specific. An example in use in a local school at the time of writing is shown in Fig. 8.2.

Practical assessment	
Date:	
Year:	
Investigation title:	
Class:	

Group	Pupils:
A	
B	
C	
D	
E	

	Dependent variable What are they measuring?	Measuring instruments What have they chosen? Are they suitable?	Range and accuracy Range of readings? How accurate?	Independent variable What are they changing?	Control variables What are they keeping the same? Is it a fair test?
Group A					
Group B					
Group C etc.					

Fig. 8.2 Assessment sheet

Experience suggests that checklists such as this are most appropriate to the teacher who is learning how to make judgements by highlighting the criteria against which those judgements will ultimately be made. Eventually, as the teacher gets to know the class and becomes more confident in both the teaching and the assessment of investigative work, the list becomes less important and may be used only to record unexpected happenings.

Pupils' written work

Much information can be gleaned from the pupils' written work. The use of prompt sheets (see Fig. 7.1) can also aid the assessment because pupils are more likely to record the salient information. However, not all of the pupils' written information can be relied upon. This is not necessarily because pupils wish to cheat. They often fail to write down what they see as trivially obvious things which may be revealed when they are asked to describe what they have done. More seriously, evidence shows that they can claim, in good faith, to have controlled a variable while in reality having failed to do so. The misunderstanding of the notion of the fair test (as in Jonathan's report; see p. 104), for instance, can also easily mislead the assessor unless supported by observation. It is here, perhaps, that the checklist in Fig. 8.2 serves its most useful function.

An example of a pupil's written report (Melanie's group) serves to illustrate the extent to which evidence can be accumulated. The pupils had already been introduced to the particulate nature of matter. The task was set in the context of a rapid turnover drinks stall, but the teacher, in an oral

---

Melanie's group

Experiment: To find out which sugar dissolves fastest.

What we need: Caster, granulated and demerara sugar, warm water, stopclock and stirring spoon.

What we did: We measured 4 ounces of each sugar, put them in a beaker with 100 ml of water and stirred them until they dissolved and put the results in a table.

What we kept the same:

1 The amount of sugar
2 The amount of water
3 The amount of stirring

Results:

Sugar	Time
Caster	1.35
Granulated	4.34
Demerara	7.02

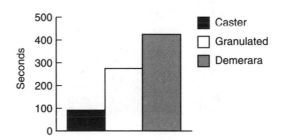

What we found out:

We found out that caster sugar was the fastest to dissolve.

Sarah's group (aged 11)

Plan

I am going to find out if the material of the cup affects how fast it cools down.

I think the cup which is thick will hold the most heat because there will be more material for it so it wouldn't be able to escape through the side.

I am going to change the different material of the cup and take the temperature after they have cooled down to see which is hotter.

Type of cup	Amount of chocolate	Temp. when hot	Temp. when cold
Polystyrene	45	90	60
Plastic	45	90	58

Report

I got all my equipment together and put 4 spatulas of hot chocolate in 2 kinds of cups which were polystyrene and plastic. I put the boiling water in the cups and took the temperature which was 90°C in both of them. Later when they were cooling down we took the temperature again.

The heat was a bit hotter in the polystyrene cup than in the plastic one because the polystyrene is thicker. It took quite a long time to cool to the temperature we got when it was cooling.

Tentative ideas of energy transfer (heat loss) and insulation are being used to come to a prediction – though they are not clearly formed.

She changes the type of cup – though only picks two materials out of a range of four available. She measures the temperature with a thermometer but does not measure the time at all.

At first sight it appears that Sarah has carried out a fair test. She certainly knows that she should – by keeping the temperature the same at the start, and the amount of chocolate powder used. However, she did not measure the amount of water in the cups and it was in fact different. She has not actually carried out a fair test although she recognises one.

Results are presented clearly in a table and used to come to a general statement linked back to the original question. She displays her results in a bar chart and realises that the final temperatures are not much different.

Discussing this with her, she realised that she had not put the same amount of water in each cup and that this might help to explain why she had not really got a reliable difference in her results. Fair testing is not just about keeping 'something' the same – but knowing the importance of controlling certain variables.

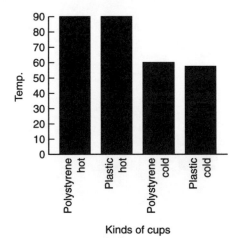

introduction, stressed the importance of providing scientific evidence on which to base a judgement.

Melanie's written report shows that she has a clear understanding of design; she has selected the key independent and dependent variables and clearly stated how she controlled the relevant control variables. The measurements appear to be accurate, although this is best confirmed by observation. The scale of her design is appropriate, but she does not mention repeating any measurements. Her presentation of results is sensible, but she does not relate dissolving time directly and explicitly to the underlying concept of grain size, which was the teaching context in which the investigation arose.

Another example, with a commentary and in a different context, shows how a pupil's written record can be misleading.

Planning vs performing

Can procedural understanding, as deployed in investigations, be assessed using tasks in which pupils are asked to plan an investigation rather than actually do it? Clearly, the answer has to be 'yes'. Any plan for an investigation must have considered the relevant elements of skills and procedural understanding. But it is important to realise that it is quite a different kind of assessment. Some evidence from APU work illustrates this difference clearly.

The APU gave pupils investigations in two written forms – one in prose and the other using pictures. They also asked other pupils to actually carry out the same investigation. The results showed that the pupils were far more successful on the practical than on the written questions (Table 8.4).

They were also more successful with pictorial clues than with the question in prose alone. The APU also asked the same pupils to do similar tasks in a written and practical form. The previous results were confirmed. It follows that if pupils are successful in the written question, then they are likely to be successful in the practical investigation. The main point here is, however, that children who do not write adequate plans can still perform well in the practical situation.

Strang *et al.* (1991), following Gott and Murphy (1987), explain this striking difference in performance as due to the interaction with the apparatus in the practical situation. In the written form, pupils have to imagine the apparatus and design the investigation in the abstract. There is also little scope for trial and error. In the practical situation, pupils can revise and change their plans as they proceed. This does not imply that written plans are of no value. Indeed, Strang *et al.* (1992) suggest that written plans can be a useful starting point for discussion of strategies for investigations.

Questioning

Questioning will give vital diagnostic and summative information at all points. In the assessment situation, the questioning of all groups may seem impractical but can be limited to a few carefully

Table 8.4 Examples of practical *vs* written responses to an investigative task (Strang *et al.*, 1991)

Which fabric would keep you warmer?

		% pupils		
		Prose	Pictorial	Practical
Control of variables:	Volume of water	6	9	51
	Conditions of cooling	21	44	60
Use of measuring instrument:	Stopclock	1	18	80
	No measurements made	54	31	17

focused questions to test the understanding of particular concepts of evidence, which is not always apparent either in the observation or in written accounts. Probing pupils' understanding of particular ideas can be carried out using shorter follow-up assessments. An example focusing on data interpretation including the concepts of evidence of patterns and a fair test is shown in Fig. 8.3. This information is likely to be diagnostic and formative rather than summative.

Dissolving – data interpretation

Karl and Lee

Karl and Lee did the same investigation as you. This is what Lee wrote:
First of all we set everything up and we had a beaker with water.
We put 3 heaped spatulas of sugar in a beaker and timed it.

Sugar	Time to dissolve
white	65 sec
brown	84 sec
icing sugar	65 sec

We found out that icing sugar went fastest because the bits of brown sugar were bigger.

1 Is there anything wrong with Lee's conclusion? What is wrong?

2 Do you think they carried out a fair test? Why do you think that?

3 What do you think they really found out?

Susan and Vicky

This is how Susan and Vicky presented their results

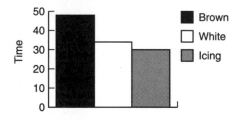

This is how Susan wrote her report:

We set up our materials and put 200 ml of water in a beaker. We tipped the sugar in. We had 2 ml of sugar. We started to stir. We were timing while stirring. When all the sugar had dissolved, we stopped the clock. The brown sugar took longer. Brown sugar is harder than icing sugar. That's why it took longer.

4 Do you think Susan and Vicky carried out a fair test? Why do you think that?

5 Who do you think wrote the best description of what they did. Lee or Susan? Why do you think that?

Fig. 8.3 A follow-up exercise on data interpretation (Gott *et al.*, 1993)

Pupil self-assessment

The idea of pupils assessing themselves raises the spectre of pupils awarding themselves at least as many marks as their closest friend, and probably one more. The reality is very different. In schools where this approach has been tried, it has been found that most pupils are their own greatest critics. They are unreliable as sources of evidence.

But the notion that mark schemes should be secret docs not equate with the idea that pupils have a right to know – and indeed should know – what is expected of them rather than having to guess what is in the assessor's mind. Making the assessment targets clear, or as clear as possible, through a self-assessment sheet, has the advantage of providing an agenda for instant feedback, and hence converts the assessment into a learning situation as well. Self-assessment sheets can also serve as 'prompt' sheets for pupils when they are writing reports of their work.

An example of a self-assessment sheet which focuses on concepts of data handling and evaluation is given here. It is specifically designed to encourage pupils to use their results rather than spending too long saying what they did: an altogether less demanding exercise and, hence, more popular!

It is clear that these assessment sheets can be designed and used to focus on the relevant concepts of evidence which are being assessed by the teacher. For example, the assessment sheet could be more tightly focused on design by restricting its headings, if that is to be the focus of a particular task. The teacher must also be aware of the difficulty of language that we have referred to elsewhere in this book, so that some time should be spent on 'teaching' pupils what the statements mean as well as how to use self-assessment, to give them confidence in completing the sheets. The exercise is intended to promote pupils' understanding of their own progress as well as being a useful assessment tool for the teacher.

Making judgements

The overview

Whatever the form of assessment, the methods we have described can contribute to an overview (Fig. 8.4) which can be used to generate the 'raw data'. Each method of assessment can contribute in different ways to the overview. The pupils' interpretation of the data and their ideas on the reliability of their data and on the validity of their investigations is often not made explicit in their written accounts but may be elicited by careful questioning. The self-assessment sheet can also serve as a guide while pupils are writing their reports. Experience suggests that controls, scale, the choice of instrument and accuracy are best assessed by observation. Assessing their ability to produce reliable and valid data is a more complex exercise. It can only be done by reference to all the evidence. Valid data require that pupils have identified the correct variables and that there are no serious systematic errors in their experi-

---

Assessment sheet
Investigation title:

My level is (good, very good) because I have shown that I can:

• decide what to change	
• decide what to measure	
• decide what to keep the same	
• choose the best measuring instruments	
• take measurements over a wide range	
• repeat measurements for accuracy	
• carry out a fair test	
• record my results clearly in a table	
• draw and label a graph	
• get information from my graph	
• describe patterns in my results	
• explain my conclusion using scientific knowledge	
• EVALUATE how my results are useful, only if I have done a fair test	
• suggest DIFFERENT interpretations of my results	
• describe step by step what I did	

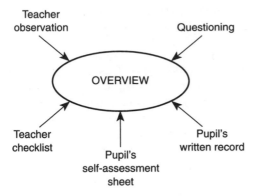

Fig. 8.4 The informed overview of the assessment of investigations

mental design. Reliability depends on accuracy and repeatability, which in turn depends on the choice of instrument and the accuracy with which it is used, the number of readings taken and so on.

Table 8.5 suggests the *principal* source of evidence for each of the concepts.

Norm-referenced and criterion-referenced assessment

Before we can look at how the information can be used to inform judgements, we must take a brief sidestep into the issue of norm- and criterion-referencing in the context of summative assessment. In planning an assessment we must consider what sort of information is required from that assessment. We shall consider two basic ways of dealing with the accumulated data about pupil performance.

The first is based on the addition, somehow, of 'marks' for any particular action that was 'correct'. This method resembles the task and interpretation scores described on pp. 55–6. By adding these marks in various ways, particular strengths and weaknesses – in broad terms at least – can be revealed. Thus, for instance, if we wanted to see if a class had grasped the concepts associated with the design of investigations, we might assess the performance of children by adding the number of points that they achieved in the design section

Table 8.5 Principal sources of evidence

		Observation supported by checklist and self-assessment sheet	Written work	Questioning
Design	Identified key variables as independent and dependent variables correctly		√	
	Appropriate variables controlled for fair test	√	√	
	Variables identified as categoric or continuous (as appropriate)		√	
Measurement	Scale – quantities chosen sensibly	√		
	Range – quantities spread over an appropriate range		√	
	Instruments chosen and used appropriately	√		
	To give suitable accuracy	√	√	
	Measurements repeated if necessary		√	
	Appropriate sample size (if relevant)		√	
Data handling	Table used to organise data collection		√	
	Graph chosen (or omitted) as appropriate		√	
	Data interpreted correctly		√	√
	Link to reality included in interpretation		√	√

only. This kind of assessment will give data suitable for putting pupils in a 'pecking order', either for the whole or parts of the investigation, the traditional norm-referenced approach.

The second way, criterion-referenced assessment, involves using the checklists and pupils' work to make judgements against particular criteria. The issue of criterion-referencing will be deferred until the next chapter where we look at the National Curriculum in the UK, which purports to be an example of this method of assessment.

The understanding of individual concepts of evidence within investigations

In a traditional norm-referenced assessment, the 'domain' to be assessed is defined and a series of tasks set to sample that domain. The resulting score is then taken to be representative of ability within that domain. In our case, the domain is that of procedural understanding. The more tasks used, across a greater spread of concept areas and contexts (both everyday *vs* scientific and open *vs* closed), the greater the validity and reliability of the score.

Using simple task scores

Table 8.6 gives a summary of the sort of data that could be collected for assessment. It would be drawn, as we have argued earlier, from a variety of sources: observation, pupil records and so on. It can be seen from the table that the additive task score is easily obtained. The disadvantage of this type of score is that any failure at an early stage does not preclude getting a 'mark' at a later stage, so that two children obtaining the same score may have performed very differently and be able to apply quite different concepts of evidence. The breakdown of the task score into the broad categories of design, measurement, data handling or evaluation can be more meaningful in pinpointing broad areas of relative strength or weakness. Additive scores, however, take *no* account of how the concepts of evidence relevant to the investigation are put together.

Nobody would think it sensible to carry out a driving test by assessing, with the car stationary and the engine off, whether the driver knows how to drive by looking at the mechanics of changing gear, using the brake pedal and so on.

Table 8.6 Using the task score and its components in assessment

	Overall view			Assessment report	
Design	Identified key variables as independent and dependent variables correctly	√		Task score	9
	Appropriate variables controlled for fair test	√		Design	3
	Appropriate sample size (if relevant)			Measurement	3
	Variables identified as categoric or continuous (as appropriate)	√		Data handling	2
Measurement	Scale – quantities chosen sensibly	√			
	Range and interval appropriate				
	Instruments chosen and used appropriately	√			
	Measurements repeated				
	To give suitable accuracy	√			
Data handling	Table used to organise data collection	√			
	Graph chosen (or omitted) as appropriate				
	Pattern in data recognised, interpreted and linked to reality	√			

What matters is, can he or she *drive*? If the driving as a whole is judged to be imperfect, then it may be useful to ascertain why by assessing individual components of the process. The key here is the realisation that in a complex activity such as a scientific investigation, the whole is far greater than the sum of the parts, which leads us to the assessment of that whole – the synthesis of skills and concepts of evidence.

The synthesis of concepts of evidence within investigations

We have argued throughout this book from the standpoint that the ability to understand concepts of evidence and hence be able to synthesise them into a task solution is the ultimate goal of investigative work. But how can this synthesis be assessed?

We have argued that the notion of evaluation and its related ideas of validity and reliability are the key to all other concepts of evidence, since these concepts encompass all of them and which determine the progress of the whole task. If these ideas of validity and reliability are understood, pupils will make sensible choices of variables, variable types, data requirements and interpretation.

To assess the synthesis of pupils' investigative work, teachers need to use the overview described in Table 8.5. In the light of all this information, the teacher must then decide whether or not:

- the question has been answered (validity)
- the data are 'good', e.g. have they been collected in sufficient quantity and with appropriate accuracy? (reliability)

This judgement, based on the extent to which an objective observer would believe any conclusions, can be used as the basis for assessment. Quite how that could be done in a reliable and straightforward fashion is a matter which can only be tested in the classroom. Attempts to do so can be successful, but there is a learning curve as indicated by this extract from a discussion with a head of department:

I think that trying to pin down the assessment of 'synthesis' is very, very difficult. Like in English – you can give separate marks for spelling, sentence construction, paragraph usage and so on. But how do you give marks for imagination, unity of style? Or in art, you can give separate marks for draughtsmanship, use of colour or composition. But the overall piece of writing or the finished picture is much more than this. It is a subjective judgement, but you can try to be more objective about the bits. So what art teachers have always done is to decide for themselves, come to a consensus and then have their judgement moderated.

Unless and until all science moderators are willing to make judgements like this, science teachers will be floundering because, unlike arty types, they like things to be cut and dried. And what they need to see is that there is something else to science that they have missed along the way as they become ever more logical and nit picking in their training. There is that 'certain something' which makes an investigation better than others, and that comes from practice with checklists and things. There are certain indicators of quality – a results table is one such, variables and fair test are others, and then, above all, the idea of believability.

No doubt there will be some who will feel such an approach, itself, is not very scientific. It is all right, they may argue, for arts teachers to adopt this approach relying, as it does, on teachers making judgements and then coming to a consensus on the judgements through discussion. But in science, we must have evidence, preferably in the pupils' own writing. That, we would argue, is to confuse science with its assessment. Science relies on objective evidence; indeed, the thesis of this book is that such evidence is undervalued in schools. But assessment is not a science, even when it is applied to science. It is an art.

But we fail to accord that art the status it merits. How often do we hear that teachers have under (or over) estimated pupils' ability compared to the exam? This question assumes that the exam is correct and that the teacher is wrong. Discrepancies between teacher judgement and 'objective' external assessment are far more likely to be examination error for individual pupils, or a bad day, or questions that they didn't grasp properly. The comment should really say 'the exams have under (or over) estimated pupils' ability compared to the judgement of the expert teacher'.

If we go down the line of a more subjective, but informed, judgement, we must have some criteria against which to make that judgement. The quotes above were made in the context of the National Curriculum in the UK which is, in theory, criterion-referenced and will be treated as a case study in the next chapter.

Summary

In this chapter, we have suggested how investigations can be used to assess procedural understanding and how information from a variety of sources can be collected prior to making the final assessment. A key decision that has to be made by any assessor is whether that judgement is to concentrate on individual concepts of evidence or their synthesis. The former allows for a more traditional pattern of aggregating 'scores' in that marks for each concept of evidence can simply be added. The latter relies on a more subjective approach which, while relying on the same evidence, seeks to stand back and come to an overall judgement which allows for the fact that an investigation is more than the sum of its parts. This, we believe, is more in keeping with the spirit of investigative work.

References

Coles, M., Gott, R. and Thornley, T. (1988). *Active Science 1*. London, Collins Educational.

Coles, M., Gott, R. and Thornley, T. (1989). *Active Science 2*. London, Collins Educational.

Gott, R. (1993). *Investigative Tasks for Assessment*. Durham, University of Durham.

Gott, R. and Murphy, P. (1987). *Assessing Investigations at Ages 13 and 15*. APU Science Report for Teachers No. 9. London, HMSO.

Gott, R., Welford, G. and Foulds, K. (1988). *Assessment of Practical Work in Science*. Oxford, Blackwell.

Gott, R., Price, G. and Thornley, T. (1991). *Active Science 3*. London, Collins Educational.

Gott, R., Costello, H. and Foulds, K. (1993). Materials to support the assessment of Sc1. Draft document, Durham University.

Northern Examining Association (1992, 1993). *GCSE Chemistry: Syllabus A*. Manchester, NEA.

Strang, J. (1990). *Measurement in School Science*. Assessment Matters No. 2. London, SEAC/EMU.

Strang, J., Daniels, S. and Bell, J. (1991). *Planning and Carrying Out Investigations*. Assessment Matters No. 6. London, SEAC/EMU.

CHAPTER 9

Investigations and the UK National Curriculum

In the previous chapter, we looked at various ways of collecting evidence for assessment purposes and making judgements which reflect different emphases. The UK National Curriculum presents us with a different problem. It is premised on a criterion-referenced system of assessment which revolves around a set of criteria (the Statements of Attainment) within a curriculum defined by the Programmes of Study (DES, 1991). The curriculum is essentially assessment-driven, which is why we are dealing with it in this chapter.

Criterion-referenced assessment, if it deals with trivia, is relatively easy to operate (Gipps, 1992). For instance, whether or not a pupil takes a thermometer out of its case before using it could be a criterion. But it is hardly vital, except of course in that particular and localised instance. If the criteria are to refer to something more generally significant, then they inevitably become more judgemental in nature. The real question, then, in constructing the National Curriculum, has been that of determining at what level of generality these criteria are to be and how judgements are to be made against them.

The National Curriculum has included investigations in the curriculum since its formal inception in 1989. This official recognition of the significance of investigative work in science education is an innovative move which has been influenced, in part, by the work of the APU and later by the recommendations of the Task Group on Assessment and Testing (TGAT) report (DES, 1988a).

The overall structure of the National Curriculum for science has been modified considerably since it was introduced. By looking briefly at these changes, we shall see how the present structure of the National Curriculum has evolved and the thinking behind the definition and assessment of the investigative component.

The development of the National Curriculum

The National Curriculum which was proposed in 1988 consisted of twenty-two 'Attainment Targets' (ATs) for science. These attainment targets remain, although they have been reduced in number. They are simply descriptions of things which pupils should know, understand or be able to do. Each attainment target is then divided into ten levels defined by 'Statements of Attainment' (SoA), through which pupils can progress from the ages of 5 to 16. These statements of attainment are intended to act as the criteria in a criterion-referenced system. The twenty-two attainment targets in the original version were grouped together for the purposes of reporting, into four *profile components*:

1 Knowledge and Understanding (ATs 1–16)
2 Exploration and Investigation (ATs 17 and 18)
3 Communication (ATs 19 and 20)
4 Science in Action (ATs 21 and 22)

The National Curriculum was originally intended for formative as well as summative assessment purposes. The very nature of the twenty-two attainment targets, with their very detailed criteria, was most appropriate for formative assessment to guide future teaching and learning. Its early structure was heavily influenced by the work of the Assessment of Performance Unit (APU), which was charged with assessing the *system* through the pupils, rather than assessing the pupils as individuals. The confusion between the assessment of a system, which requires merely that pupils are sampled, and assessing pupils summatively resulted in fault lines. A system designed to measure populations was used, indeed abused, to assess individuals. Readers are referred to Gipps (1992) for further discussion.

The assessment, then, came to be used in a summative way because the assessment results were to be summarised for publication by schools for the so-called 'league tables'. In this way, schools could be publicly compared in terms of the attainment of their pupils. So we have the paradoxical situation of a criterion-referenced system, designed largely for diagnostic and formative purposes and relying heavily on teacher judgements, being asked to produce relatively simplistic norm-referenced information to put *schools* in a 'pecking order'.

We will look below at the development of these criteria in relation to investigative work. It will be noted that the original criteria have become drastically reduced in number and, hence, increased in their level of generality. They have, then, become more like descriptions of a domain than a set of criteria to be met.

If we look more closely, we can see the role of investigations (Profile Component 1 as it then was) in this original version (Table 9.1).

It can be seen that Profile Component 1 was a mixture of skills, concepts of evidence, substantive concepts, and observation. Profile Component 2, 'Communication', also included some concepts of evidence. Table 9.2 gives some examples.

Both these profile components include many of the concepts of evidence which we have suggested are at the heart of procedural understanding, but they are mixed up with other aspects of science. The message as to what, precisely, investigations were to be used to assess was far from clear.

The proposed structure consisting of twenty-

Table 9.1 Profile Component 1: Exploration and Investigation (DES, 1988b)

- Explore events and phenomena seeking regularities and noting the unexpected
- Formulate hypotheses which can be tested experimentally
- Plan and carry out investigations using apparatus, materials and methods appropriate to the problem being investigated
- Make and systematically record observations which are relevant to the problem being investigated
- Represent experimental findings using graphs, tables, charts, symbols and conventions as appropriate
- Select measuring instruments which are suitable to a task and use them to an appropriate level of accuracy
- Recognise variability and unreliability in measurements
- Make inferences and justify them in the light of the data
- Evaluate the design of experiments
- Use a range of measuring instruments
- Estimate quantities
- Follow instructions in verbal and written form
- Work with an awareness of safety aspects
- Treat living things with respect

Table 9.2 Profile Component 2: Communication (DES, 1988b)

- Represent experimental findings using graphs, tables, charts, symbols and conventions as appropriate
- Use secondary sources, including the media, other people, reference books, databases and select information relevant to a particular topic of study
- Translate information between graphical, tabular, pictorial and prose forms
- Communicate information on a scientific topic to others in written and oral form
- Consider alternative theories, hypotheses and models (including personal theories) and assess their claims in relation to observations and other evidence

two attainment targets, each of which was to be assessed, was soon found to be too complex and unwieldy as the move from a sampling idea and teacher assessment was replaced by the requirement to assess all pupils on all aspects of the Programme of Study. In December 1988, a consultation report recommended reducing the attainment targets to seventeen, within two profile components:

Profile component 1 (Attainment Target 1)
Exploration of science, communication and the application of knowledge and understanding.

Profile component 2 (Attainment Targets 2–17)
Knowledge and understanding of science, communication, and the applications and implications of science.

(NCC, 1988)

This recommendation was implemented in March 1989. A further reduction was proposed in 1991 (NCC, 1991) and implemented soon after. The attainment targets were now reduced to four and the term 'profile components' subsequently abandoned. This structure applies at the time of writing, although there are already signs that it may change again.

The present National Curriculum

The shrinking of the curriculum, together with the fact that teacher assessment has been reduced, has meant that it can no longer claim to be formative assessment, at least in the terms originally defined. It is now akin to a traditional 'sampling knowledge' type examination and hence primarily summative in nature. Its purpose has become largely one of accountability.

So how do investigations and procedural understanding fit into 'today's' National Curriculum? The four attainment targets currently are Investigations (Sc1), Life and living processes (Sc2), Materials and their properties (Sc3) and Physical processes (Sc2). Attainment Target 1, scientific investigation, is defined within the Programme of Study, as follows:

Pupils should develop intellectual and practical skills which allow them to explore and investigate the world of science and develop understanding of scientific phenomena, the nature of theories and procedures of scientific exploration and investigation. This should take place through activities that require a progressively more systematic and quantified approach which develops and draws on an

increasing knowledge and understanding of science. The activities should develop the ability to plan and carry out investigations in which pupils:

(i)   ask questions, predict and hypothesise
(ii) observe, measure and manipulate variables
(iii) interpret their results and evaluate scientific evidence

(DES, 1991)

These three components or 'strands' form the basis of the assessment.

Strand (i) brings in the substantive concepts of science in the 'raising of questions' or hypotheses (Table 9.3). This poses a number of problems. Principally, of course, it represents an attempt to assess the substantive structure of science which is already covered by Sc2–4. Over and above that, it is very difficult for pupils if the hypothesis is seen as being the source of any investigation. Experience shows that it is hard enough for any of *us* to generate questions suitable for investigations which will target skills and concepts of evidence in any sort of coherent fashion.

In Strand (ii), Table 9.3 shows that the lower levels are concerned with observation but from level 3 to level 9 concepts of evidence concerned with design and measurement appear. Level 10 includes evaluation. Strand (iii) is a conflation of data interpretation and evaluation of evidence and the drawing of inferences based on that evidence (Table 9.3). The first locates within concepts of evidence; the second, once again, moves into the substantive concepts of ATs 2–4.

How does this assessment relate to our view of the content of procedural understanding? If we draw out the concepts of evidence as they appear in the levels of the curriculum (Table 9.4), we can see that while most are included, some such as repeatability or sample size are not mentioned specifically in any of the strands.

Like the original version, the overall picture of assessment in Sc1 is rather confused. On the one hand, it seems to be assessing some concepts of evidence, while on the other hand, it is about applying substantive concepts. There appears to be no clear underlying philosophy. It is based around the 'doing' of practical activities rather

Table 9.3 Strands in Attainment Target 1: Scientific investigation in the National Curriculum (DES, 1991)

Pupils should carry out investigations in which they:

Level	Strand (i) Ask questions, predict and hypothesise	Strand (ii) Observe, measure and manipulate variables	Strand (iii) Interpret their results and evaluate scientific evidence
	Pupils should carry out investigations in which they:		
1		(a) observe familiar materials and events.	
2	(a) ask questions such as 'how...?', 'why ...?' and 'what will happen if ...?', suggest ideas and make predictions	(b) make a series of related observations	(c) use their observations to support conclusions and compare what they have observed with what they expected
3	(a) suggest questions, ideas and predictions, based on everyday experience, which can be tested	(b) observe closely and quantify by measuring using appropriate instruments	(c) recognise that their conclusions may not be valid unless a fair test has been carried out (d) distinguish between a description of what they observed and a simple explanation of how and why it happened
4	(a) ask questions, suggest ideas and make predictions, based on some relevant prior knowledge, in a form which can be investigated	(b) carry out a fair test in which they select and use appropriate instruments to measure quantities such as volume and temperature	(c) draw conclusions which link patterns in observations or results to the original question, prediction or idea
5	(a) formulate hypotheses where the causal link is based on scientific knowledge, understanding or theory	(b) choose the range of each of the variables involved to produce meaningful results	(c) evaluate the validity of their conclusions by considering different interpretations of their experimental evidence
6	(a) use scientific knowledge, understanding or theory to predict relationships between continuous variables	(b) consider the range of factors involved, identify the key variables and those to be controlled and /or taken account of, and make qualitative or quantitative observations involving fine discrimination	(c) use their results to draw conclusions, explain the relationship between variables and refer to a model to explain their results
7	(a) use scientific knowledge, understanding or theory to predict the relative effect of a number of variables	(b) manipulate or take account of the relative effect of two or more independent variables	(c) use observations or results to draw conclusions which state the relative effects of the independent variables and explain the limitations of the evidence obtained
8	(a) use scientific knowledge, understanding or theory to generate quantitative predictions and a strategy for the investigation.	(b) select and use measuring instruments which provide the degree of accuracy commensurate with the outcome they have predicted	(c) justify each aspect of the investigation in terms of the contribution to the overall conclusion
9	(a) use a scientific theory to make quantitative predictions and organise the collection of valid and reliable data	(b) systematically use a range of investigatory techniques to judge the relative effect of the factors involved	(c) analyse and interpret the data obtained, in terms of complex functions where appropriate, in a way which demonstrates an appreciation of the uncertainty of evidence and the tentative nature of conclusions
10	(a) use scientific knowledge and an understanding of laws, theories and models to develop hypotheses which seek to explain the behaviour of objects and events they have studied	(b) collect data which are sufficiently valid and reliable to enable them to make a critical evaluation of the law, theory or model	(c) use and analyse the data obtained to evaluate the law, theory or model in terms of the extent to which it can explain the observed behaviour

Table 9.4 Concepts of evidence in the National Curriculum

Concepts of evidence (not in any particular order)	Level at which they appear (in strand 2 unless noted)
Identifying variables as independent and dependent	3 (strands 2 and 3)
Fair test and control variables	3
Categoric, discrete and continuous variables	3
Scale	
Range	5
Accuracy	6
Choice of instrument	4
Repeatability	
Variation, sample size and probability	
Tables	
Choice of graph type	
Recognising and interpreting patterns	4,5
Interpreting multivariate data	7
Validity	3,9
Reliability	9,10

than the *understanding* that underpins that activity. It is no wonder, then, that its implementation has been fraught with problems. Some teachers who are unsure about assessing the 'content' of procedural understanding, focus on the assessment of the application of substantive concepts, with the result that the understanding of concepts of evidence becomes marginalised. Others see it as no more than traditional practical work as before.

The issue of whether the assessment is about individual concepts of evidence or their application and *synthesis* is also unclear. On the one hand, the curriculum emphasises that assessment is to be carried out 'in the context of complete investigations' (SEAC, 1993). While on the other, the suggestion is that the three strands be assessed separately within the context of whole investigations:

All of the abilities that pupils need to demonstrate have therefore to be assessed in the context of whole investigations. This does not mean that each investigation has to offer the opportunity to assess all three strands. Nor does it necessarily mean that where an investigation allows all strands to be assessed, the teacher has to assess them all. It may be more manageable to record a pupil's performance on each strand in the context of different investigations.

(SEAC, 1992)

So while there is clear guidance to use whole investigations for assessment, confusion reigns over whether to focus on individual concepts of evidence or their application and synthesis.

The research evidence and the present curriculum

Strand (i) asks pupils to generate their own hypotheses to test. Many teachers see this, not unreasonably, as the starting point. But there could hardly be a more open start. As a consequence, some pupils will ask questions that are incapable of being answered at all, or certainly not with the apparatus available. But more importantly, they will tend to ask questions, the solutions for which are already within their grasp. As we saw in the research, the move to open questions led pupils to regress to a more qualitative solution. Such an approach is not going to bring out the best in pupils, which surely we should be aiming for.

The emphasis on conceptual understanding across strand (i) – and strand (iii) to a lesser extent at the higher levels – makes heavy demands on pupils. As we have seen in our research, the effect of the concept area on performance is one of the most influential factors. The assessment of procedural understanding will be, to all intents and purposes, impossible if the biggest hurdle for pupils is conceptual. The existing National Curriculum attempts to structure progression on variable complexity. There is a clear thread defining the required independent variable(s), which suggests a progression from the type 1 investigations (as defined in the research) to type 2 to types 3 and 4. The research has demonstrated that this order is consonant with assessing application and synthesis.

At the same time, pupils are being asked to apply concepts at a level commensurate with the level of Sc2–4:

There should be approximate parity between the level at which pupils are working in Sc1 and the level of knowledge and understanding in Sc2, 3 or 4 needed to make appropriate predictions or hypotheses (strand i) and to make sense of the outcomes (strand iii).

(SEAC, 1993)

The requirement that the concepts should be the same or at a similar level to that of the investigation is to ask pupils to apply newly acquired understanding of substantive concepts *and* concepts of evidence. This fundamental problem remains. The research reported here, and the increasing criticisms levelled by teachers, suggests that such an approach is untenable, elevating as it does the higher levels of Sc1 into what one teacher has described as a PhD thesis. Sc1 must refocus itself on the procedural understanding which sets it apart from Sc2–4. As our much quoted head of department says:

Getting the pupils to raise a question themselves, writing perfect plans, relating their conclusions to scientific knowledge and so on are all very worthy things to do, and I try to do them. But they get in the way of pupils showing their procedural understanding and should be assessed separately. They are the points at which teachers get bogged down and pupils get discouraged because they can't do all the bits perfectly and stay at one level. The insistence on [the substantive concepts being part of assessment as well] is hindering investigations taking off properly. And if that looks as though I am ignoring how concepts fit in with investigations, I am not. That is where the scheme of work is so important.

Add to that our often reiterated comment that the research, and the underpinning of the National Curriculum, is biased towards quantitative work and we begin to see that, as it stands, the structure has its problems but is well worth building on. Time will be needed for it to develop. So we should be looking for ways of improvement; two possible ways forward are suggested below.

The ways forward

A structure based on the complexity and sophistication of evidence

Of prime importance in any revision is to recognise that a wholesale rewriting is simply not possible at this particular stage; the system above all needs time to settle in. But what is also quite clear is that a philosophy must be provided if some coherent progression is to be built into the criteria. One possible way of structuring progression based on a 'content' of procedural understanding which attempts to reflect the existing structure of the curriculum is shown in Table 9.5. We have used the existing ten-level scale as our starting point; the criteria could be used in a number of different ways, one of which we shall explore in a later section. We have also tried to keep the levels as close as possible to the existing ones, not because we believe them to be necessarily correct, but for purely pragmatic reasons in that continual tinkering is causing teachers to lose that trust necessary for the investment of time and effort in new schemes of work. It is also worth noting that the structure is, we suggest, only a part of any revision which might well include elements connected with skills, written assessments based on data interpretation and the nature of evidence in science and engineering.

This structure (Table 9.5) is based on the complexity and sophistication of the evidence planned for, generated and interpreted within the task. There are a number of advantages to this approach: crucially, the basis is one of *understanding, application* and *synthesis,* rather than skills or any other sort of 'doing'. The assessment is then of a complementary nature to conceptual understanding, revolving around *concepts of evidence,* which are the content descriptors of that understanding.

The *complexity* of the evidence relates to the type, number and complexity of the variable structures in an investigation. A task involving continuous variables, for instance, gives both more data and more

Table 9.5 Levels defined by the complexity and sophistication of the evidence

Level	Key indicator *Within a complete task:*
4	Carry out a complete task which will give data that answer the original question
5	Recognise the importance of a fair test and of the scale and range of the values involved in ensuring that the resulting data are 'believable'
6	Use continuous data to represent a pattern and the relationship of that pattern (in a line graph) to scientific understanding
7	Disentangle the effect of more than one independent variable
8	Use patterns to predict what will happen and collect data of appropriate scale, range and accuracy to allow the prediction to be checked
9	Synthesise evidence from a variety of sources (multiple investigations or a mixture of investigations and use of secondary sources) into a coherent argument and conclusion
10	Understand the interplay between theory and evidence, the use of evidence to test a theory or the use of theory to check the reliability and validity of evidence

complex data as the need for range and accuracy linked to patterns comes into play. The *sophistication* of that evidence depends on the concept(s) (and context) which underpins it. We have noted that, for instance, the connection between a pattern in data and the reality of the event that they represent is a crucial element of science.

The *tasks* themselves are not defined so they are not limited by variable structures because it is the outcome, in terms of evidence, that is defined. Tasks of other kinds which generate complex and sophisticated evidence can be used, such as simple qualitative analysis in chemistry where the logical structuring of the task based on the accumulation of evidence is paramount (Table 3.6 gives some examples of other types of investigative work).

The key indicators of progression in Table 9.5 can be seen as pegs along this path of increasing complexity and sophistication (it is limited to levels 4 and above, those most relevant to secondary schools). It will be apparent that they represent the pupils' ability to put together a strategy for the complete task and so are based, as we argued in the previous chapter, largely on ideas of validity and reliability.

Using the criteria

How can these key indicators (Table 9.5) be related to the present National Curriculum? We suggest using these key indicators as the initial criteria against which to locate a pupil's investigation. Teacher judgement is essential here. The existing criteria at that level can then be used as supporting criteria to assist in making a judgement as to whether the pupil has or has not met, *more or less*, the criteria related to and defining the level. This may seem a very subjective approach, but the search for objective criteria is bound to fail. Complex understandings are not capable of unambiguous definition when limited to a few statements.

In reality, this is criterion-related judgement rather than strict criterion-referencing and as such it must be based on case law. Experience suggests that, given a set of criteria and some examples of pupils' work, judgements can be brought into line *and* increase teacher understanding of what is required.

Another point of some importance in using criteria of any sort, including our suggestions here, is the degree to which the statements are to be interpreted in a legalistic sense. In the existing assessment structure of the National Curriculum, pupils' work is judged against level 1 (for instance) and if it meets all those requirements it is judged at level 2, again compared to every single phrase within the criteria. And so on. Clearly, the effect is cumulative. In the end we find ourselves looking for evidence at level 10 that pupils (in one piece of work?) have met every single criterion that has gone before, all twenty-seven of them. And so nobody can succeed.

There is another way. We can look at a pupil's work and match it against key indicators with a view to finding the *best overall match*. Then the additional criteria can be used to make an overall judgement as to whether the work is sufficiently close to that level, *as a whole*. This may seem like a hair-splitting exercise, but the change in stance from working upwards through all the words of the statements to a judgemental matching is not to be underestimated. Level 10 then becomes something which can be judged over a number of pieces of work using the criteria as canons of judgement rather than legalistically interpreted hurdles. As the head of department quoted before says:

> I find having to obey the 'letter of the law' of the NC criteria discouraging. It needs putting right. Using judgements seems a revolutionary way of assessing, but it is 'do-able'. You *stand back* from the pupil's work and you have the criteria (manageable – not too many fine details) in your mind clearly before you start – then you exercise your judgement. It is a clearer and more relaxed way of assessment. The 'nit-picking' approach is essential for details of conceptual understanding. It is *not* the way to judge procedural ability.

It will be noted that there is no reference to science concepts (the substantive elements) in these suggested criteria. The reason is tied to the interplay between context and concepts which the research shows plays such a big part in determining pupil performance. The concepts and contexts are largely set by the Programmes of Study defined for each key stage. These, quite rightly, differ from stage to stage. The consequence of that is, of course, that a pupil in Key Stage 3 will be assessed on an investigation set in contexts defined by the Key Stage 3 programmes of study and using concepts that are within their grasp. A pupil attempting *the same level* in Key Stage 4 would come across a different set of concepts and contexts. The level of demand will be quite different. As the Dearing Report (1993) notes:

> This [the problem of the 10 level scale] raises the question of whether, for example, the level 3 in history achieved by a bright Key Stage 1 pupil means the same thing as the level 3 achieved by the less able 14-year-old [in relation to the completely different programme of study].

The sensible thing, then, is to define levels within a key stage based in the concepts of that key stage,

rather than attempt a too grandiose and all-encompassing set of criteria. One suggestion is shown in Table 9.6. The range covered and degree of overlap is an arbitrary choice. All that is required is a recognition that the assessment is to be of the ability to generate, understand and use evidence in the context of investigations set within the contexts and concepts *defined by the Programme of Study*. The grades, be they letters corresponding to GCSE grades or labels such as average, above average and so on, will then be qualified by the key stage at which the assessment is made.

The Dearing Report (1993) suggests something similar: 'One possibility for the end of key stage assessment would be a five (or six.....) point grading in each of the Key Stages 1 to 3 leading on to the General Certificate of Secondary Education scale at Key Stage 4.'

In the introduction to this chapter, we suggested that the level of generality of criteria and the problem of how judgements are to be made are the major problems. Our suggestions above can only be seen to deal with these questions if:

- the criteria, which are still very general, are given meaning through many examples or tasks and examples of pupils' work; and
- the various ways of collecting evidence suggested in the previous chapter are used to form judgements against those criteria.

Other strands

The above amounts to a structure based on one factor – the idea of evidence. We regard this as the central feature of Sc1, but a broadening of the definition to include skills, data interpretation and, potentially, the nature of scientific evidence might be considered. Certainly at Key Stage 4 there is a place for more advanced skills that involve the more sophisticated instruments encountered at that level. This would build on the progress made in GCSE work within the National Criteria, which was proving popular before its demise at the hands of the National Curriculum. It would also provide a vehicle for inclusion of tasks which are essentially based on 'finding a way' to measure

Table 9.6 A norm-referenced approach to levels

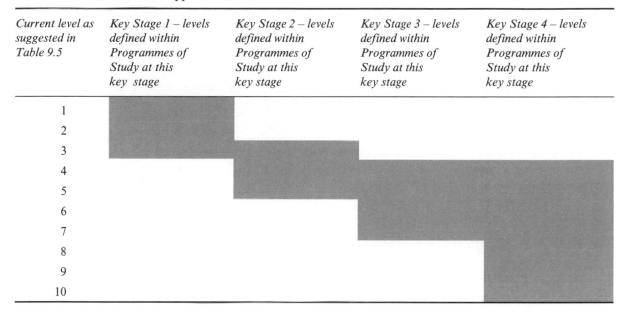

Current level as suggested in Table 9.5	Key Stage 1 – levels defined within Programmes of Study at this key stage	Key Stage 2 – levels defined within Programmes of Study at this key stage	Key Stage 3 – levels defined within Programmes of Study at this key stage	Key Stage 4 – levels defined within Programmes of Study at this key stage
1				
2				
3				
4				
5				
6				
7				
8				
9				
10				

Table 9.7 Possible strands for a new structure for Sc1

Strand (a)

Carrying out investigations	Designing tasks and collecting valid and reliable evidence

Strand (b)

Skills	Use of apparatus and measuring instruments and the interpretation of evidence from primary and secondary sources

Strand (c)

The nature of evidence in science and engineering	Empirical evidence and its relationship to laws and theories and as a predictor of the behaviour of materials and systems

something, often a key element in science. We have seen examples in earlier chapters of activities based on individual concepts of evidence; the NEA core skills paper is one example of that approach in practice. Such tasks could also form the basis of a strand based directly on the interpretation of 'second-hand' data.

Inclusion of a strand linked to the nature of science itself has some attractions, particularly when we remind ourselves of the data presented in Chapter 4, which showed the disparity in teachers' perceptions of practical work in science. Its successful incorporation would rely on it not becoming confused with the history and philosophy of science, which tends to focus on historical discoveries or ideas about inductivism or falsification. We mean nothing so grand for pupils at this age. We do believe that the current provision fails to prepare students, particularly those going into engineering, to encounter empirical evidence which does not have any formula to attach to it. For example, graphs in civil engineering often are envelopes within which the material is likely to behave. To a student of school physics who expects a graph to 'prove' some law or other, this can be a significant hurdle to learning. Whether it can be incorporated into a workable assessment system in an area which we have shown still is on a steep learning curve is open to doubt. The strands then might become as shown in Table 9.7.

A structure based in a norm-referenced framework

A quite different alternative is to use the taxonomical structure in the way it is used in conventional examining practice. A typical examination planner will begin by creating a grid for assessment objectives and content. We give a much simplified version in Table 9.8.

The grid will encompass all the assessment objectives and all the content areas. Then, rather than attempt to cover all the boxes in the examination, questions are distributed around the grid to reflect the overall weightings of the objectives. There may

be more questions in the understanding row, fewer in the application and fewer still in the recall. This grid, then, represents the *domain* which is to be assessed and the results obtained from the sampling of that domain are used to give an estimate of a pupil's ability in the subject defined by the domain.

Exactly the same approach can be adopted for a domain of procedural understanding. The grid now contains 'concepts of evidence' rather than substantive concepts but in other respects the issue is identical (see Table 9.9).

Questions can now be distributed across the grid, making sure that there is a spread of concept

Table 9.8 An assessment planning grid for (substantive) concepts

Assessment objectives	Electrical current	Voltage	Energy	Etc.
Knowledge and recall of skills				
Understanding of concepts of evidence				
Application of skills and concepts of evidence (in unfamiliar situations)				
Synthesis of skills and concepts of evidence (in problem-solving)				

Table 9.9 An assessment planning grid for procedural understanding

Assessment objectives	Skills	Define variables	Fair test	Sample size etc.
Knowledge and recall of skills		▓▓▓	▓▓▓	▓▓▓
Understanding of concepts of evidence	▓▓▓			
Application of skills and concepts of evidence (in unfamiliar situations)				
Synthesis of skills and concepts of evidence (in problem-solving)				

areas. There will be some skill tasks, written and practical, some short tasks based on individual concepts of evidence and some practical investigations. It will be remembered that a key feature of investigations is their ability to differentiate by outcome, so it will be possible to use relatively few such tasks to cover a wide spread of ability. And, just as for traditional examining, marks and weightings can be allocated to each question and a final total used to represent ability in that domain. We give this alternative as a technical example rather than as something we would advocate.

GCSE assessment of Sc1

As the final touches were being put to this manuscript, the suggestions for assessment of Sc1 for GCSE were dropping through school letterboxes. The method being adopted by the Northern Examining Association (NEA) is of some interest in the light of the above arguments. They suggest that assessment be carried out using whole investigations and that the level be defined in relation to 'key features': 'An investigation needs to be of the right type according to these descriptions [the key features] if the mark for each skill [strand] is to be awarded' (NEA, 1993).

So the first step, they suggest, is to decide at what level the pupil's work is compared to the key features before deciding on what to do about any one skill (strand). Then, the assessment calls, implicitly, for teachers to use their judgement: 'It is now possible for these assessment criteria to be used in such a way that a candidate can be awarded a mark without necessarily having satisfied each and every one of them in full.'

So, having decided on the overall level, the teacher is being asked to judge if each skill (strand) has been attained, whether or not every single element of that strand has been 'ticked'. Another suggestion made above, that pupils' work should be matched against criteria by looking for a 'best overall match', is paralleled in the NEA documents: '...the criteria should be used to identify *best fit* between the work and the criteria... provided the investigation is of the right type (defined by the key features)'.

The correspondence between these suggestions and our analysis is close, which suggests that there is a convergence in meaning as to what Sc1 is about; the language is becoming established.

Summary

We have seen in this chapter how the National Curriculum has developed from a mixture of skills and concepts of evidence towards something which concentrates more directly on the synthesis of concepts of evidence. We have suggested that the insistence on the inclusion of substantive concepts with which pupils are not necessarily at home is to miss the point of the assessment, which surely is not to repeat an assessment of concepts which can be carried out more effectively in other ways. Furthermore, the evidence suggests that its inclusion denies some pupils the opportunity to demonstrate their procedural understanding.

A move towards subjective judgement based on key indicators, supported by other criteria, would, we believe, not only make assessment easier to manage in the classroom but also give a better picture of pupil ability. The most recent documents on assessment from the examining boards seem to recognise and support this view. Most encouragingly of all, perhaps, is the extent to which the language of investigations and its attendant case law is converging. This, we must hope, signals a convergence of philosophy.

References

Dearing, R. (1993). *The National Curriculum and Its Assessment: An Interim Report*. York, London, NCC/SEAC.

Department of Education and Science and Welsh Office (1988a). *National Curriculum Task Group on Assessment and Testing: A Report*. London, HMSO.

Department of Education and Science and Welsh Office (1988b). *Science for Ages 5 to 16*. London, HMSO.

Department of Education and Science and Welsh Office (1991). *Science in the National Curriculum*. London, HMSO.

Gipps, C.V. (1992). National Curriculum assessment: A research agenda. *British Education Research Journal,* 18(3) 277–86.

National Curriculum Council (1988). *Consultation Report: Science*, December. York, NCC.

National Curriculum Council (1991). *Consultation Report: Science,* September. York, NCC.

NEA (1993). *Science Framework Guidance on the Assessment of Sc1 GCSE*. Northern Examinations and Assessment Board.

SEAC (1992). *School Assessment Folder Part Two: Science*. National Pilot. London, SEAC.

SEAC (1993). *School Assessment Folder Key Stage 3: Assessing Sc1*. London, SEAC.

CHAPTER 10

Postscript

This book has explored the role of investigations in the science curriculum in the light of current research. Our central theme has been that investigations are not just another tool in the teachers' repertoire for teaching the substantive concepts of science, but a tool with a very specific purpose – that of teaching for the understanding, application and synthesis of concepts of evidence which lie at the heart of procedural understanding. We have put forward ways of teaching these concepts of evidence and of incorporating investigations into the curriculum. We have suggested ways of making investigations more meaningful to pupils by using the notion of an 'audience' for the resulting evidence.

The current science curriculum focuses primarily on substantive conceptual knowledge. We have suggested that a more balanced view of science would give greater attention to procedural understanding. The research we have presented disputes the assumption that children gain procedural understanding simply by doing practical work in the course of traditional science teaching. This common view was epitomised at a recent conference when an apparently accepted opinion was stated as: 'we know that practical work is important – but because everyone can do it, there's no need to worry about it'.

Research findings suggest that there is indeed 'something to worry about'. While it is encouraging that children can do practical investigations in the sense that they can design and collect data, it is a matter of concern that they do not get past this

point and that they do not value the significance of their own evidence. Pupils particularly lack the important parts of procedural understanding which we have defined as those concepts of evidence associated with the validation of evidence. If pupils have not been taught these ideas, then it is hardly surprising that they do not understand them. There has also been, and still is, a tendency to regard procedural understanding as something which once acquired is only useful in as much as it is a means of teaching concepts. We have argued that procedural understanding is something that is worth teaching in its own right.

We have demonstrated how the content of procedural understanding can be broken down into concepts of evidence which serve two purposes. First, it enables the teacher to examine children's performance in investigations to see which concepts children do and do not understand. Second, it means that investigations can be designed to focus on particular aspects of investigations and to teach particular concepts of evidence. The issue of the assessment of investigations is not without its problems, particularly in the UK National Curriculum. If we accept the view that the assessment of the synthesis of concepts of evidence is the goal, then assessment should ultimately rely on the informed judgement of the professional teacher.

So far, our arguments have stemmed from the research we have presented. Here we shall put forward a more personal view.

If we consider the aims of educating pupils in science, then we start from the point of view of equality of opportunity which we take as fundamental. An education system without a belief that all pupils are equally worth educating and that they deserve the same chance would be a moral failure. This does not mean that we can guarantee, or even wish to strive for, equality of output. That is up to each individual pupil. But they should all have the chance. In terms of science education, we are not talking about producing more top scientists but working towards a more scientifically literate society.

The phrase 'the public understanding of science' is much in vogue at present. It points to the fact that there is a growing awareness that there is something wrong with that understanding – that it is in need of improvement. Industry is particularly concerned that a science-trained workforce needs more 'transferable skills' at its disposal. Both these issues can be, and we would argue should be, addressed at the school level.

How then do pupils regard science? To many, it is a subject that is hard, irrelevant and boring. Added to this is the fact that science has a negative image in society generally, which is passed down from one generation to the next. We shall consider each of these claims in turn before we consider how these problems can be addressed.

Science is hard?

Assessment of Performance Unit (APU) data from the 1980s showed that something like 20 per cent of the nation's 16-year-olds could make sense of the concepts of science. In some areas of physics and chemistry, the proportion is nearer 2 per cent. It seems as if science is indeed 'too hard' for the majority. But this is well known and equally well documented:

> School science has, both overtly and covertly, become more pure, conceptually demanding and complex, and less concerned with the everyday reality and experience of our youngsters, their parents and their employers: it has, in so many ways, become a complex symbolic system accessible to the few.
>
> (ASE, 1979)

A more personal view, and one which expresses the sheer frustration felt by many of our best science teachers, is typified by this quote from a teacher in one of our research schools:

> I want people to be interested in science. None of my friends ever were. I think if it had been left to school science alone, I would definitely have followed the Arts. But my father was an engineer and he was fascinated by science and this influenced me.
>
> By the 6th form, if you thought about the science it held you back – if you learned the formulae and followed the instruction you were well away – if you could stand the boredom. Science had become dead, and dead hard.
>
> [At university], my friends did English and art and French and history; they were always being encouraged to think for themselves, analyse but give their own opinion and reasons, using the evidence they had. Would tutorials in science open up this discussion? No! – more formulae and instructions. All in all, the message was – be able to stick the numbers in the right places in the formulae, but never mind what it means.
>
> When I started teaching I decided I wouldn't teach like that, but would try to make things clearer to everybody. But in the end I felt I'd conned them into opting [for physics] because, with all the formulae and instructions, there was hardly time (or anyone with the staying power), or teaching suggestions in text books – to try to keep it interesting. I felt like force of [the teacher's] personality alone drove them to success at 'O' level, in the midst of incomprehension.

Science is irrelevant?

The criticism that school science is irrelevant is not new either:

> Although there are some impressive exceptions, too much time spent learning science by too many pupils consists of the accumulation of facts and principles which have little perceived, or indeed actual, relevance to their daily lives as young people or adults.
>
> (DES, 1985)

Unfortunately, there is a feeling in society and among some scientists that school science *is* school science and no matter whether it appears to be boring or irrelevant, you cannot fiddle about with it. This is the 'science is hard, and if they can't get into it, well so be it' approach. Whether this is the view of those who have been through science training, or the view of 'laymen' who are over-impressed by the mysticism of pure science, is arguable. The political rhetoric in some quarters seems particularly impressed with these arguments; it has the feel of 'back to basics' about it:

> The thrust in science towards practical, investigative and experimental work has left less time available for its teaching, and has undermined further the acquisition of knowledge.
>
> (Centre for Policy Studies, 1988)

This extraordinary statement beggars belief. What we can only assume, to be charitable, is that the authors have confused discovery learning with practical science. If they really believe that science is not about 'practical, investigative and experimental work', then the future for science and engineering is indeed bleak.

Science is boring?

Ideas that are difficult, set in contexts perceived as irrelevant, result in failure. Failure often leads to lack of motivation, boredom and classroom disruption. Many students leaving school science, never to return, will say that it was a set of disjointed and incoherent facts that made increasingly less sense. Foulds *et al.* (1992), in discussing this kind of fragmented teaching, write: '...this situation is likely to leave many pupils with the same sterile view of science as that which pertained during the 1960's and which resulted in few students opting for further studies in science'.

This may all sound like an attempt to place blame on the teachers. Not so. They can only teach what the curriculum asks – indeed, in the UK now instructs – them to teach. They will nearly all say that the curriculum in secondary schools is too full. There is no time to explore ideas and the consequences of science in their pupils' everyday lives. And so science stops with the school bell.

A bad image?

> Young people see science as destructive. By damaging the environment, contributing to wars and experimenting on animals, science has lost its appeal and the popular portrayal of scientists shows them as dangerous or insane.
>
> (Purchon, 1991)

Science has undoubtedly caused some of the problems in today's world but it has also found the cures to many, although the latter is not always recognised.

Another contributory factor to this negative image is that the 'objective' nature of science can be taken to imply that scientists are uncaring and

Helen Yr4

unemotional people. They are seen as somehow remote from society. The more caring image of biology drives pupils towards the biological sciences or into the arts where that humanising influence is more apparent.

Newton and Newton (1992) asked young children to draw a picture of a scientist and found as on p. 141, that many young children drew a male scientist, with a balding head, wearing a white coat and working with test tubes in a laboratory. This stereotype of a somewhat remote figure set apart from society may be acquired by as early as six years of age.

An alternative science?

To those 'in the know', science is a fascinating way of looking at and understanding the world. Many younger pupils, particularly in primary and early secondary, share this view. What can we do in schools to enable children to retain this interest?

If we look at the content of the science curriculum, then we can see a number of core ideas or key substantive concepts which are essential for scientists, engineers and technologists and indeed for the scientifically literate person. We cannot throw these key concepts away, even if they are hard. The best we can do is to keep them to a minimum and present them in a way which makes them accessible to the majority of students and in a way which highlights their relevance. But there remains a lot of clutter around these big ideas. The result of the clutter is that many *graduates* come to teacher training knowing a lot and understanding little. They are full of very erudite sounding knowledge. Ask them to explain some everyday phenomenon and the key gaps in those big ideas show through all too clearly.

When we look at procedural understanding, it is here that we find the core of 'transferable skills' that industry asks for. These transferable skills are those which make up the general scientific approach to issues which can be applied across many situations. One of the most important of these skills is the ability to evaluate evidence:

To decide between the competing claims of vocal interest groups concerned about controversial issues such as 'acid rain', nuclear power, *in vitro* fertilisation or animal experimentation, the individual needs to know some of the factual background and to be able to assess the quality of the evidence being presented.

An uninformed public is very vulnerable to misleading ideas on, for example, diet or alternative medicine. An enhanced ability to sift the plausible from the implausible should be one of the benefits from better public understanding of science.

(The Royal Society, 1985)

Evidence is, science must be central. It is the key that differentiates science from maths, for instance. In science, as in mathematics, any theory has to be internally consistent but in science it also has to be tested against reality. If it fails the test, it is, or should be, discarded. That is a pure scientist's view of evidence and one that is difficult to fit neatly into science for younger pupils.

But applied scientists and engineers rely on evidence to a far greater extent. When an engineer designs a bridge, the theory may help in understanding the problem, but it would be a foolish engineer indeed who designed a bridge in the absence of empirical evidence about real bridges. Evidence here is the rock upon which any engineering project is based and the quality of that evidence and its believability must be central. It is also more accessible to pupils in schools than the 'purer' use of evidence to test theory. Scientists in industry rely on the ability to generate, validate and interpret evidence. But most importantly, it is this evidence which will form the basis for the:

Humanising [of] the science curriculum by developing an understanding of human nature in relation to the natural environment to enable citizens to deal with problems that have ethical, value and moral components.

(Hurd, 1993)

It is the ability to evaluate evidence and to begin to appreciate such components, that we are arguing for in this book and which we believe provides the core of the transferable skills that we seek.

Turning to the issue of motivation which must be central to any development in science education, there is general agreement that investigative work engages pupils' interest. In particular, there is some anecdotal evidence that girls, the biggest source of untapped potential in science, find the open approach more to their liking. Why might that be? One suggestion that has been floated concerns the transfer of control, and ownership, to the pupil. As we saw in the quote above from the (female) teacher, she saw her fellow students at school in art subjects challenged to think, while she plugged numbers into formulae. Investigations require that sort of challenge to think. What we hope we have shown in this book is that there is a 'content', primarily of concepts of evidence, to investigative work which underpins and provides the rationale for their inclusion in any balanced curriculum.

References

Association for Science Education (1979). *Alternatives for Science Education*. Hatfield, ASE.

Centre for Policy Studies (1988). *Simple Curricula for English, Maths and Science*. Policy Study No. 93. London, Centre for Policy Studies.

Department of Education and Science (1985). *Science 5–16: A Statement of Policy*. London, HMSO.

Foulds, K., Feasey, R. and Gott, R. (1992). *Investigative Work in Science*. Durham, University of Durham.

Hurd, P.D. (1993). Comment on Science education research: A crisis of confidence. *Journal of Research in Science Teaching*, 30(8): 1009–11.

Newton, D.P. and Newton, L.D. (1992). Young children's perceptions of science and the scientist. *International Journal of Science Education*, 14(3): 331–48.

Purchon, V. (1991). A prayer for the new priest-craft. *Times Educational Supplement*, 8 November.

Royal Society (1985). *The Public Understanding of Science*. London, The Royal Society.

Index

PRACTICAL SCIENCE
THE ROLE AND REALITY OF PRACTICAL WORK IN SCHOOL SCIENCE

Brian Woolnough (ed.)

Science teaching is essentially a practical activity, with a long tradition of pupil experimental work in schools. And yet, there are still large and fundamental questions about its most appropriate role and the reality of what is actually achieved. What is the purpose of doing practical work? – to increase theoretical understanding or to develop practical competencies? What does it mean to be good at doing science? Do we have a valid model for genuine scientific activity? – and if so do we develop it by teaching the component skills or by giving experience in doing whole investigations? What is the relationship between theoretical understanding and practical performance? How significant is the tacit knowledge of the student, and the scientist, in achieving success in tackling a scientific problem? How important are such factors as motivation and commitment? What do we mean by transferability and progression in respect to practical work? – do they exist? – can they be defined? How can we assess a student's practical ability in a way which is valid and reliable and at the same time encourages, rather than destroys, good scientific practice in schools? This book addresses such questions.

By bringing together the latest insights and research findings from many of the world's leading science educators, new perspectives and guidelines are developed. It provides a re-affirmation of the vital importance of practical activity in science, centred on problem-solving investigations. It advocates the need for students to engage in whole practical tasks, in which all aspects of knowledge (tacit as well as explicit), of practical ability, and of personal attributes of commitment and creativity, are interacting. While considering the particularly pertinent issues arising from the National Curriculum for Science in England, its discussion is equally germane to all concerned with developing good practical work in schools .

Contents

Setting the scene – Practical work in school science: an analysis of current practice – The centrality of practical work in the Science/Technology/Society movement– Practical science in low-income countries – a means to an end: the role of processes in science education – Practical work in science: a task-based approach? – Reconstructing theory from practical experience – Episodes, and the purpose and conduct of practical work – Factors affecting success in science investigations – School laboratory life – Gender differences in pupils' reactions to practical work – Simulation and laboratory practical activity – Tackling technological tasks – Principles of practical assessment – Assessment and evaluation in the science laboratory – Practical science as a holistic activity – References – Index.

Contributors

Terry Allsop, Bob Fairbrother, Geoffrey J. Giddings, Richard Gott, Richard F. Gunstone, Avi Hofstein, Richard Kimbell, Vincent Lunetta, Judith Mashiter, Robin Millar, Patricia Murphy, Joan Solomon, Pinchas Tamir, Kok-Aun Toh, Richard T. White, Brian E. Woolnough, Robert E. Yager.

224pp 0 335 09389 2 (Paperback)   0 335 09390 6 (Hardback)

TEACHING IN LABORATORIES

David Boud, Jeffrey Dunn and Elizabeth Hegarty-Hazel

This is a complete guide to the design and organisation of laboratory activities and the conduct of laboratory teaching. It is an exhaustive, up-to-date account and appraisal of current practice, with recommendations for change supported by case studies.

Notoriously time and labour intensive, lab work is doubly threatened when resources run scarce. It is particularly dependent upon precise objectives, purposeful structure, effective experiments, and close assessment. This book brings together and elucidates all that has been and could yet be done in the sciences to maintain and improve effectiveness and keep lab work in the curriculum. Research and regular course evaluation in this field are shown to be essential to development.

Contents

Introduction – Aims, objectives and course planning – Teaching strategies – Sequencing and organization – Assessment of students – Monitoring laboratory teaching – Research on laboratory work – Aide-memoire for the development of a new laboratory course – References – Index.

192pp   0 335 15609 6 (Paperback)

BIOTECHNOLOGY IN SCHOOLS
A HANDBOOK FOR TEACHERS

Jenny Henderson and Stephen Knutton

In recent years there has been spectacular growth in biotechnology and in its importance for the school curriculum. This handbook offers teachers:

- an overview of the significance and scope of biotechnology
- an introduction to the content of biotechnology and its relevance to the everyday world
- a guide to how biotechnology fits into the National Curriculum, within and across subject disciplines
- appropriate teaching strategies
- suggestions for practical work
- case studies and other material which can be used directly with sixth form students
- a glossary of terms
- a guide to resources
- coverage of safety issues.

This is an essential resource for practising and trainee teachers of science and technology.

Contents

What is biotechnology? – Biotechnology and the school curriculum – Biotechnology and the food industry – Biotechnology and medicine – Biotechnology in agriculture – Biotechnology and the environment – Biotechnology, fuels and chemicals – Biotechnology through problem solving – Biotechnology through discussion-based learning – Practical considerations – Resources – Glossary – Appendix – References – Index.

176pp   0 335 09368 X (Paperback)
0 335 09369 8 (Hardback)

LEARNING AND TEACHING IN SCHOOL SCIENCE
PRACTICAL ALTERNATIVES

Di Bentley and Mike Watts

This book provides a series of different approaches to teaching school science. These approaches will be of use not only to science teachers but also to teachers outside science and in different parts of the education system.

The book is organised as follows. The first chapter looks at pressures for change: the authors show that science teachers need to adopt new and different approaches to teaching and learning. In particular, the authors focus on the notion of active learning – a theme that runs through the remainder of the book. In the following chapters, case studies are clustered around a series of themes. The final chapter summarises the approaches and their implications for teaching science for the National Curriculum.

In general, the book is a useful, practical guide to a variety of strategies and classroom activities: a collection of experience and ideas about different teaching methods which will benefit both trainee and practising teachers. It will appeal to those engaged in initial training and in-service work, as well as to teachers who are keen to innovate.

Contents

Preface – Acknowledgements – Learning to make it your own – Practicals and projects – Talking and writing for learning – Problem solving – Encouraging autonomous learning – Games and simulations: aids to understanding science – Using role play and drama in science – Media and resource-based learning – Summary and discussion – Index.

The Contributors

Brigid Bubel, Bev A. Cussans, Margaret Davies, Rod Dicker, Mary Doherty, Hamish Fyfe, John Heaney, Martin Hollins, Joseph Hornsby, Andy Howlett, Pauline Hoyle, Harry Moore, Robin Moss, Phil Munson, Philip Naylor, Jon Nixon, Mick Nott, Anita Pride, Peter Richardson, Linda Scott, Brian Taylor, David Wallwork, Norma White, Steve Whitworth.

224pp 0 335 09513 5 (Paperback)
0 335 09514 3 (Hardback)